Conversion Rate Optimization

Using Neuroscience And Data To Boost Web Conversions

BY

Dr. Ali Nasser

Copyright © 2019 Azya Publishing
All rights reserved. No part(s) of this book may be reproduced, distributed or transmitted in any form, or by any means, or stored in a database or retrieval systems without prior expressed written permission of the author of this book.

Contents

Preface vii

Part 1: Introduction 1

    Using Neuroscience to Dramatically Grow
    Website Revenue 7

    Structure Of This Book 8

**Part 2: Conversion Optimization – Currently the
Largest Digital Marketing Opportunity** 13

  2.1   Using Conversion Rates To Crush Competitors..... 15

  2.11 Competition Driving the Imperative for
        Testing and Optimization 19

        Cost Per Conversion Calculation 21

  2.2   Google Ads – A Winner Take All Example for
        Conversion Optimization 27

  2.3   ROI - Is The Juice Worth the Squeeze? 29

  2.31 Avoid Analysis Paralysis on Lifetime Value (LTV) .. 31

| 2.4 | B2B Sales Funnel Analysis, the Value of Additional Conversions .... 33 |

Part 3: Conversion Rate Optimization – Team And Process 37

3.1	CRO: A Tough Team Sport 39
3.2	Sample Size – Tests Only Amazon Can Run 41
3.3	Hypotheses Fast-Track Results and Reduce Errors 45
3.4	Organizational Challenges 47

Part 4 : Neuroscience And Data – Secrets to Conversion Optimization Success 49

4.1	Battle of the Apes (or Customers) 51
4.2	Emotion, Habit and Rational Behavior.................. 53
4.21	Human Brains Create Ideas Invisible to Marketers. 59
4.22	Applying Concepts of Influence to Design and Optimization 63
4.23	Buyer Motivation by Job Title 65
4.3	Fear Drives Decision-Making 69
4.31	Scarcity and Conversion Rate Optimization 77
4.4	Inclusion Drives Conversion 83
4.5	The Power of Social Proof 89

4.6	Emotional Needs and Attachment Driving Purchasing 95
4.7	Brain Shortcuts – The Neuroscience of Priming..... 99

Part 5: Introducing Personalization 107

5.1	Personalization - A Structured Approach to Conversion Optimization and Segmentation/ Multivariate Testing 109
5.2	Evaluate Whether Personalization Is Worthwhile . 117

Part 6: Data-Driven Decision-Making in Testing 119

6.1	Funnel Analysis and Drop Off 121
6.2	"The Price Is Right" 125
6.21	The Neuroscience Of Price Perception And Testing 131
6.22	Pricing, Segmentation and Upselling 139
6.3	What Drives Willingness To Pay 141
6.31	Differentiated Offers Command Value 143
6.32	Presentation Driving Conversion 145
6.4	Neuropricing and Measuring Willingness to Pay .. 147
6.41	The Neural Mechanisms Implicated in Willingness to Pay 149

6.5   Leveraging Neuroscience 151

6.6   Brain Imaging, And Conversion Optimization 153

Concluding Thoughts.. 157

Acknowledgments 159

About the author.. 161

Preface

My Journey Toward Understanding the Brain, Human Behavior, and Design

I spent my undergraduate studies focused on the brain and its impact on human behavior. My coursework encapsulated all of the different elements of neuroscience and how we learn and interact with our environment. This included neuroanatomy, neurophysiology, hormones and behavior, various psychology classes, genetics, and biology. This multifaceted program grew into a lifelong obsession with understanding how we make decisions and how to influence those decisions.

One fascinating course, titled "Hormones and Behavior," was aptly described by the professor as a study of *"Hormones, Sex, and Aggression."* The class revealed that much of animal and human behavior can be studied in the context of these two primary instincts: sex and aggression. There is compelling evidence that animal studies contribute to our understanding of human behavior, the brain, and biology. While we can consciously decide what to do or not do, ultimately, we cannot deny our underlying biology.

As part of my education, I approached one of my professors for a position in his lab. His studies focused on the field of psychophysics and the study of the relationship between stimuli and sensation. For example, we might study how a person interpreted a stimulus, like turning sound into a musical score, and learn a new scoring algorithm embedded in the software. While this is a gross simplification of the lab's research, the example study explored the conscious and unconscious process of translating a signal to a response. The team discovered that people are very often influenced at the subconscious level.

I became fascinated with consciousness and the influence of the unconscious mind on decision-making. With the encouragement of my professor, I was able to explore and embrace its nebulous nature. I was intrigued by dynamic consciousness and the use of quantum physics and its potential relationship to human consciousness. The comparison is interesting, given that our thoughts are far from linear and cannot be explained by classical mechanics. From there, I explored chaos theory, which looks at how small changes can extensively impact systems. The classic example is a butterfly's wings flapping, potentially causing a hurricane in another part of the world. Theories are interesting but not often useful in the real-world. Rather, they helped create a path for me into the exploration of the human mind.

There are situations where one can study decision-making and actually watch it occur at subliminal rather than conscious levels. Human beings in research studies can tell the difference between the weight of objects subconsciously, despite not being able to discern the difference at a conscious level. Human instinct influences decision-making on a deeper level than our conscious function.

This early interest in the study of the mind predates the internet and the field of consumer neuroscience. While still a relatively young discipline, neuroscience is vast in comparison to its application to online user experience. Applying the idea to the study of human behavior, relevant to neuroscience and the internet, raises inherent challenges. A significant portion of the challenge is the attempt to measure elements of human behavior that may not have established analytical metrics. It can be difficult to examine results using purely scientific methods.

Researchers are held to high standards in study design, statistical methodology, and peer review. It is hard to imagine a digital marketer conducting a similar type of study. For example, it would appear to be overkill to write a report on the methods of a particular analysis the way scientists do in research papers. That being said, I have found myself wondering how the field of user experience and design could benefit from more rigorous and comprehensive approaches.

For example, scientists routinely discuss the challenges involved in recruiting study subjects for research purposes. These methodological challenges are very relevant to the research studies and are critical to any publication in a relevant scientific journal. In the online world, there are no requirements for any such analysis. Often, market research is done with minimal attention to these issues. The issue is lesser in many A/B tests where two versions of a single page are compared using randomly assigned visitors. The random assignment ensures an adequate control group and permits a similar statistical analysis to that conducted in research studies. That said, digital marketing could benefit from learning more about the scientific method, statistics, and conclusions drawn from relevant large-scale studies on human behavior and interaction.

Part 1

Introduction

Conversion Rate Optimization, the Retail Apocalypse, and the Cure for Cancer

Most digital properties have the intention of generating a lead, phone call, sale, or action of some kind; this action taken by a web visitor is called a conversion. While companies spend billions driving traffic to websites and other digital properties, there is relatively little investment being made into increasing the number of people that convert.[1] Testing different versions of web pages and deploying better performing 'winners' in a systematic manner is often referred to as conversion rate optimization (CRO) or A/B testing.[2] CRO often holds the key to a company's success.

---

1 Digital spend alone is ~$100B per year in the US, but almost all marketing spend drives traffic to digital properties. A/B testing software sales and services combined are far less than 5% of this number.
2 A/B testing is a specific type of test. Conversion optimization refers to the broader exercise of increasing conversion rate, most often through systematic testing of an entire digital customer journey.

The retail apocalypse refers to the mass closure of large traditional brick and mortar retailers as a result of an inability to compete with strong digital brands like Amazon. Many household names that were the cornerstone of the American retail landscape like Macy's, Foot Locker, GAP, The Limited, Abercrombie & Fitch, Children's Place, Payless Shoes, and others have closed thousands of stores, some filing for bankruptcy.

This failure to compete begs the question: where did these companies go wrong with their online strategy. There are two components of online success:

1. Driving traffic
2. Converting that traffic into customers

Companies can often solve the traffic acquisition side with a single, expert individual for each source of digital traffic, along with an adequate budget to fund the traffic acquisition. However, the second component, onsite conversion, is something that most brands have failed at and suffered the consequences.

There are estimates that most of the top 50 sites are neglecting to employ more than 30% of known best practices.[3] If sites with

---

[3] Team analysis, proprietary data

hundreds of millions in revenue are not able or willing to look at existing benchmarks to improve their sites in 2019, they will be assured of their place on the list of endangered retailers. A similar trend holds true for business to business (B2B) companies, where startups face ferocious competition. If you Google terms related to cybersecurity, you find companies bidding hundreds of dollars per conversion to a sales lead. Companies that invest intelligently into conversion optimization will be the winners of the digital acquisition competition.

The impact of not optimizing the opportunities presented online is far reaching. When companies develop new medications, they must recruit patients, very often using the online channel. Imagine how many patients could benefit from being in a research study, many of which are free and treat rare diseases. Consider how much society could benefit if we could accelerate the pace of approvals by enrolling the right patients into the right trials. Most patients research their illnesses online, where there are abundant opportunities to view the details of novel therapies for their cancer, but they often fail to convert from web visitors into enrolled patients.

For one customer, we were able to increase conversion rate by 58% for a leading pharmaceutical company with a single test. The company we worked with was targeting a relatively uncommon type of cancer (pancreatic cancer) and was concerned about their ability to enroll a sufficient number of patients into their clinical trial. Furthermore, my team was able to repeat this level of improvement with other drug trials, in relatively rare cancer types. In each case, the team was able to assist the company with completing its clinical trial enrollment. This enabled the company to generate the required data for submission to the FDA, which is part of the process of gaining eventual drug approval. Looking at digital marketing campaigns and predictive data, our team estimates a potential two to fourfold performance improvement opportunity in most patient recruitment digital campaigns. This result can be achieved within just a few months of optimizing paid media campaigns and landing pages. The opportunity for improvement is far greater in this industry than others, where the digital marketing skill sets are scarcer and where compliance and regulation are difficult to overcome.

Many research studies fail to enroll the patients required in a timely fashion. In general, most clinical trials fail to hit their enrollment goals. According to Covance, one of the largest contract research organizations in the world, 10% of clinical trial sites fail to enroll a single patient. It turns out, only 3% of cancer patients sign up to participate in clinical trials, but you can bet almost all of these patients are searching online for potential therapies. This is occurring despite the growth by a factor of 20 in immuno-oncology drug trials that are enrolling patients. If patients fail to sign up for trials, not only do they not gain access to therapy, but the field loses out on innovative treatments. Ultimately, a trial can only be completed if patients participate.

Using Neuroscience to Dramatically Grow Website Revenue

Imagine using neuroscience and data to eliminate the guesswork from conversion optimization.

This book tackles the concept of converting potential customers into taking a desired action on a digital property. The action may be a click, a purchase, a form fill, a download, or other valuable conversion event. The medium could be a company website, mobile app, or other digital engagement. In order to pursue conversion optimization, we need to explore some of the basics behind the metrics we use to test and optimize digital experiences. This includes examining the statistics behind experiments to determine if changes to an experience impact conversion rate. The goal is to describe how data can explain why human beings behave the way they do on a website, and then implement changes that positively influence the decision to convert.

Structure Of This Book

This book is focused on giving digital marketers an overview of the science of improving web user experience and then proposes a framework for thinking about digital marketing in the context of data and neuroscience. The high-level insights presented are derived from running tests with millions of customers. The concepts are relevant to anyone seeking to optimize their website conversion rate.

In the next section, we'll dive into why conversion optimization is potentially the largest digital marketing opportunity, how to evaluate the potential opportunity for an individual company, and why conversion optimization is a competitive necessity: companies that invest will dominate their markets, while those that fail to invest will likely perish in the evolving digital environment. Additionally, this section explores how to calculate the impact from testing using a simple, pragmatic, calculation for customer lifetime value, and the potential return on investment.

Next, in Part 3, we investigate the structure of a team and process that will accelerate a company's path to conversion optimization success. We will outline the key functions required and some of the challenges involved in building a team. The initial steps of constructing a strategy are limited by data, so we will uncover how to use hypothesis-driven testing to mitigate some of the statistical issues related to sample size and statistical significance (one of the largest misconceptions people have about testing).

Following this, Part 4 dives into the key to all conversion optimization programs: how to better understand customer buying behavior, how to evaluate motivation, and how these insights translate into user experience, design, and testing. Customers are simply human beings, so evaluating motivations and the way people think is critical in order to discern how to drive additional conversions. Again, the concept is to better understand the customer for the sake of strong hypothesis generation, which is the foundation of any testing program. Specific examples of buyers and their potential motivations are explored, which then directly translate into testable marketing messages. We review some core concepts, such as risk aversion, fear, inclusion, and social proof as additional motivations with direct value to conversion optimization and testing. These concepts are then layered into tangible examples both online and offline to drive the points home.

In Part 5, we delve into the meaty issue of personalization. There are intrinsic issues to personalizing web content, so we investigate a pragmatic path to tackling the subject and propose a structured approach to personalization. The use of examples to illustrate the potential opportunity and its application facilitates this discussion. Pragmatically, the issue that some sites may not benefit from personalization is discussed.

The final section, Part 6, examines data-driven decision-making. Here, we touch on funnel analytics and then dive deep into the topic of profit maximization and pricing. We explore issues related to how increases in profit can be driven by understanding how consumers perceive price and value, as well as demand curves, price elasticity and profit maximization. Further, we explore opportunities to upsell customers, as well as how and why they are effective. We then utilize both online and offline examples to illustrate the concepts. The neuroscience of pricing is then covered, focusing on practical examples that illustrate how to translate the discussed principles into tests. We also touch on advanced neuroimaging technology and its application to user experience testing and optimization.

The concepts laid out in this book can be powerful in enabling growth. It is important to note that, with the power to understand and influence the human mind, comes a responsibility to consider if the choices being made are ethical and will be perceived as such by others.

If we understand how the subconscious mind reacts, we may be enticed into taking an action that is discriminatory or somehow marginalizes groups or individuals. For example, if we test an image using a specific ethnicity, and it tests poorly compared to an image using different ethnicity, we may be tempted to make larger assumptions. This may be particularly true, given that we all have inherent biases based on our own background and experience.

The pictures of OJ Simpson in Figure 1 are from two leading publications. One displays a genuine picture of him, while the other one shows him as a darker-skinned man. The altered, darker-skinned image, aimed at driving additional sales, landed *Time* magazine in a great deal of trouble. Media images today are often consumed online rather than in print media, but the ethical responsibility and potential backlash remain.

Figure 1: *A side by side comparison of pictures of OJ Simpson. A darkened picture of OJ Simpson was used to sell more magazines.*

Part 2

Conversion Optimization – Currently the Largest Digital Marketing Opportunity

2.1 Using Conversion Rates To Crush Competitors

Netflix offered $1 million to improve the user experience of their onsite experience – that is, increase its conversion rate – the number of people that take an action that has value on its digital properties.[4] Companies with the best teams and technology understand that in order to win the digital game and compete, they must leverage the world's best talent. While the $1 million contest was sensationalized, it actually underestimates the amount of benefit some companies make when improving conversion rate. While Netflix's focus was on increasing the conversion rate of existing customers to engage more deeply with its product, the concept should be considered broadly: today's winners will think robustly about increasing conversion rate at all stages of the buyer journey.

Ultimately, digital marketers compete for similar groups of customers. There are a finite number of opportunities to purchase digital traffic. There are only two ways to drive more conversions for any site:

1. Increase traffic
2. Increase conversion rate

---

[4] On September 21, 2009, Netflix awarded the $1M Grand Prize to team "BellKor's Pragmatic Chaos."

Online marketers are familiar with driving traffic to their websites from a variety of channels, but conversion rate optimization (CRO) is as important. Lots of traffic with no conversion is unsustainable.

Consider a company doing $10 - $20 million in annual online revenue. Each 1% increase in conversion rate results in an additional $100 - $200 thousand in annual revenue. Over three years, that could be $500 thousand per 1% increase in conversion rate. A single conversion rate increase of 3% could easily generate $1 million in additional revenue. For a company the size of Netflix (>$15 billion in revenue in 2018), investments of $1 million or more are a drop in the bucket. Table 1 shows some examples of impact on a business with varying degrees of online revenue and lift in conversion rate from testing and optimization.

Online revenue	Conversion rate lift achieved	1 Year Impact	3 Year Impact
$5M	10%	$500K	$1.5M
$10M	5%	$500K	$1.5M
$20M	5%	$1M	$3M

Table 1: Potential impact from increases in conversion rate

It is important to consider that design and experience improvements that are empirically tested and based on a fundamental understanding of a customer can have a long standing impact. If you learn that people are terrified of purchasing shoes from you because they believe the product may not fit, then that concern is unlikely to change. Once you test an improvement to the site based on this insight, 12 months later the issue and solution are likely still relevant. Customer issues do evolve over time, but strong hypothesis driven testing will yield lasting impact to a site's performance.

2.11 Competition Driving the Imperative for Testing and Optimization

Today's digital world represents an industry where sophisticated minds can make their fortunes. There are a continuous number of new entrants into any profitable online market. New competitors can drive traffic to their sites with the help of venture capital, private equity, or reinvestment from other profitable businesses.

Over the past two to three years, there has been a massive rise in the cost of paid media that drives website traffic. This is a direct result of the rising competition for the same pool of online customers. On Facebook, for example, where marketing is done by audience segment (e.g., mothers aged 30 - 40), the increased spending of all consumer-focused marketing has driven some companies off the platform. Companies that once had profitable businesses acquiring and converting traffic from Facebook are now faced with higher costs per click and can sometimes no longer afford to compete for the traffic.

Take the example of the cybersecurity space, where thousands of new companies are operating, and the cost per click in Google Ads (formerly AdWords) is often $10 or more. A conversion to a lead may take 50 clicks or more, which means that it could cost a company $500 or more to acquire a lead. Increasing a site's conversion rate by 10% reduces marketing costs by 10%. The money would allow the site to plough that 10% savings back into the cost per click campaign, increasing the volume of traffic for the same level of spend. Higher conversion rates allow for either savings or reinvesting into acquiring more traffic.

Cost Per Lead = (Cost Per Click) × (Number Of Clicks Per Lead)
Cost Per Lead = $10 (CPC) × 50 Clicks = $500

Cost Per Lead (CPL)	Cost Per Click (CPC)	Increase in Conversion Rate	Number of Clicks Per Lead
$500	$10	0	50
$450	$10	10%	45

Table 2: Cost Per Lead Calculation

Note the virtuous cycle here: increasing conversion rates on a site can both reduce the number of clicks required to obtain a lead and reduce the cost per click. Meanwhile, site relevancy and quality increase in the eyes of Google or other platforms. The better a site or landing page converts, the lower the cost per click to drive the same traffic. The highest converting sites can spend the most on a per click basis because they are able to monetize the traffic more effectively than competitors. The better a site converts, the more that can be reinvested back into its campaign.

Let's take another example of competitive bidding on banner ads or display advertising. If a $10 click converts at 2% for Site A but 4% for Site B, then Site B can spend twice the amount that Site A can ($20 per click) and have the same cost per conversion. This is because each click converts twice as often for B versus A.

Cost Per Conversion Calculation

Site A = ($10 per click) × (50 clicks per conversion) = $500

Site B = ($20 per click) × (25 clicks per conversion) = $500

The cost per conversion is $500 in each case, so if both sites monetize their traffic equally, Site B will have a strong competitive advantage. This advantage will translate into Site B capturing a disproportionate share of the available traffic in that keyword or target segment. The highest bidders (Site B in this case) capture the most conversions through better and more frequent ad placement. The lower bidders get pushed down in ad position and frequency, resulting in fewer and fewer impressions, clicks, and conversions.

In the above example, Site B will bid up the ad price above Site A's maximum bid and effectively drive them out of contention over time. Some companies use a second site or brand to capture more clicks by holding both the number one and two positions for impressions on a page. In this example, Site B might own similar sites (X, Y, and Z) and use them to systematically dominate the market. This type of jockeying creates a fierce competitive struggle in the online arena.

Competitive bidding occurs across all media channels. Google, Facebook, LinkedIn, as well as affiliate networks, are all driven by competitive bidding of some kind.

Consider the following example. The maker of a specialty lingerie product line for young women has to compete with all other makers of products in their target demographic. In this instance, the maker of specialty lingerie may find itself outbid when competing within this demographic. If the lingerie manufacturer depends on marketing through Facebook exclusively, at some point they may fail to be profitable because their main source of traffic becomes more expensive each day.

Ironically, sometimes costs are driven up by newbies or thoughtless digital marketing efforts. There is a saying: online bidding costs are as high as your dumbest competitor. Imagine novice online entrepreneurs setting up websites to sell goods, then throwing money at advertising channels without the appropriate measurement. This then leads to overbidding for keywords, which in turn leads to higher cost for all players.

A very common issue is an agency buying digital media on behalf of large corporate customers. Suppose that an agency is hired by a Big Pharma company that bids for keywords in Google for its cardiac product. The pharma company's expertise is not in digital marketing, and the agency may have little incentive to provide results (i.e. fees increasing with the amount spent, not on results) but is required to spend all of the available budget provided by their client. Now, let's say that a small startup is promoting cardiac tracking software for people on heart medication. This company may have intersecting keywords with the Big Pharma company and compete directly for expensive keywords with bid amounts that far outstrip their ability to pay. This is the unfortunate reality in many internet markets and makes the competitive landscape ferocious for newcomers. Not all agencies are poor performers; there are some amazing digital marketers in agencies. However, not all agencies effectively manage their client's advertising budgets. Thankfully, there are many ways to compete in these situations, but increasing costs are a part of the digital landscape.

The issue is compounded by the fact that venture capitalists (VCs) are investing billions of dollars in new, high-growth businesses, driving up costs across all digital marketing channels. As a result, there are fewer sources of inexpensive traffic.

These VC-backed, high-growth companies are tasked with never ending demands to add customers as quickly as possible. They are not necessarily concerned with their immediate profits, but rather with the long-term potential of the business. Indeed, many of these businesses do not reach profitability until after their IPO (initial public offering), which could be far down the road. Many companies can remain unprofitable, even after the IPO, and retain high market capitalization.

While in hyper-growth phase, these companies must find any possible angle to push customer acquisition to new heights. Their existence and company valuation is a function of their growth rate, not just their size and profitability. They lose any lofty valuation as soon as their growth slows. These companies need to report growth metrics to the board regularly and may be asked how they might spend more money if it were made available. This might sound like an exciting proposition, however, it is challenging, even for seasoned digital marketers, to continue to grow at rates expected by investors after they have tapped out on the major digital marketing channels. There is only so much traffic to buy, and the highest quality, highest converting traffic is well-known and very competitive.

Consider a company that is currently generating 500 leads per month. They get 50% of their leads from Google Ads, 25% from LinkedIn, and another 25% from other channels like Capterra. Beyond these channels, there really is no other big lever for growth through digital channels alone.

The story is similar for high-growth businesses in the consumer space, except that the social channel is likely Facebook. All companies have the same challenge: there is no major traffic channel that is unexploited. Often, the only lever left for growth is conversion rate.

2.2 Google Ads – A Winner Take All Example for Conversion Optimization

Let's take a look at Google, the biggest advertising platform. The difference in click share (the number of clicks an advertiser receives) between the first and second position in Google Ads is usually >100%. Over time, higher converting sites can disproportionately outperform competitors by gaining enormous leads in market share, as well as reducing marketing costs. Imagine if your site could convert at a level that enabled it to capture twice the volume of traffic as your next competitor. Evidently, conversion matters to digital marketing success. Similarly, if competitors have double the traffic that you do, it can eventually lead to a significant competitive disadvantage.

One benefit of looking at Google is the transparency and size of data that they have from existing marketing campaigns. As discussed above, higher converting online experiences enable digital marketers to drive more conversions and pay more per click as a result. Google assesses a site's quality score and bid to determine how to rank their ads. There is a direct relationship between conversion rate, the ability to outrank a competitor, and capturing more traffic from a Google Ads campaign.

To Google, a site's match to a user's search is constantly assessed. This matching forms the quality score for a set of keywords. For example, if we conduct a Google search for the term "cybersecurity for email," we see ads that Google deems most relevant to our search. This is based on quality score and the amount that a site is bidding. A lower quality score can be mitigated by a higher bid, however, this results in a higher overall cost per click and cost of acquisition.

Quality score is Google's method of assessing the relevancy of a paid ad. It is based on a number of factors, not all of which are disclosed by Google. Suffice it to say that Google monitors all of the major metrics related to web experience to make an assessment. The simplest metric is measuring the relevancy of the keywords on the landing page. If there is a high relevance, then the quality score should be higher; if there is a lower relevance, then the quality score will be lower.

Other factors, such as bounce rate, are likely factored in. Google can see the behavior of visitors, and assess whether they found what they were looking for by examining how much time the user spent on the site. The quality score metric is not always a fair metric for relevancy. Nevertheless, it may be related to the conversion rate and is important when competing for valuable keywords.

2.3 ROI - Is The Juice Worth the Squeeze?

It is critical to understand how much investing in conversion optimization could impact a business. In other words, what is the return on investment (ROI) from engaging in the optimization exercise?

In order to understand the value of conversions, we must first understand the value of a customer. There are many discussions of Customer Lifetime Value (CTLV) online, some of which are quite involved and complex. A basic model and some estimates can help clarify this understanding.

The simplest method of calculating customer lifetime value is to start by understanding the following:

1. How much will a customer spend in a year?
2. What is the cost of serving this customer?
3. How long do we expect to keep this customer?

The formula is simply the profit expected in a year from a new customer (customer revenue - customer cost) multiplied by the average number of years a customer remains with the company.

If a new customer will spend on $50 on average, and the total cost, including shipping, credit card fees, and returns, is $30, then the profit is $20. If the new customer will purchase two times a year for two years on average (four total purchases), then a new customer is worth $20 × 4 ($20 profit per purchase with two purchases per year for two years), or $80.

If an annual software subscription is priced at $100, the cost of this subscription is negligible, and customers are retained for three years, then customer lifetime value is $300 (($100 − $0) × 3).

This is a very basic analysis. A more detailed analysis includes such things as discounting the value of cash received in the future, accounting for different customer segments and their buying patterns, changes in products or pricing, etc. It is best to keep this analysis simple and pragmatic in order to quickly understand the profitability of online marketing expenditures.

2.31 Avoid Analysis Paralysis on Lifetime Value (LTV)

One common error made is mistaking gross margins and net margins. This is the difference between evaluating overall business profitability versus evaluating what new customers are worth. Confusing the two can lead to lumping in additional costs when calculating the value of a new customer. If you apply all of your overhead costs to each transaction (e.g. staff, rent, electricity, etc.), then your margin will shrink, and you will make far more conservative marketing investment decisions. This is common and incorrect thinking. If you already have fixed overhead costs such as office space, heating and electric bills, and accounting staff, and you sell an additional item, then that item contributes its gross margin (product sale price minus the cost of the product) to your business. There is no need to factor in overhead costs into this additional sale for the purposes of evaluating marketing initiatives. Operating costs are the costs of staying in business regardless of a 10% increase or decrease in sales from conversion improvement or any marketing initiative.

It is true that increasing the customer base can cost money. If you dramatically grow sales and need to hire staff to service them, that is an actual cost. Factor those costs in later.

For B2B marketers and lead generators, the formula is a little bit different. Since they focus on the value of a lead, it is typically calculated based on how often a lead is converted. If a lead turns into a customer 10% of the time, then every ten leads results in one customer, and the value of a lead is 1/10th the value of a customer (CTLV × 10%). In this case, selling a product with a $100 profit and an average of two sales per customer per year over two years, the customer lifetime value is $400 ($100 × two sales per customer × two years). If it takes ten leads to get one sale in this scenario, then a lead is worth 10% of the final sale or $40 ($400 LTV divided by ten leads per closed deal).

2.4 B2B Sales Funnel Analysis, the Value of Additional Conversions

In software sales and other business to business (B2B) sales, one typically has a few steps in the marketing funnel between the online lead and closing the sale.

1. MQL - Marketing qualified lead. Marketing generates and evaluates leads as qualified (likely to become a customer), and they are passed to sales.
2. SQL - Sales qualified lead. Sales evaluates the quality of an MQL and accepts the lead for further development.
3. Opportunity - Leads that the sales force has clearly qualified as a potential opportunity. They are vetted and likely to execute a deal in the short term.
4. Closed deals - A customer that results in a sale.

It is possible to assess how often leads will result in an MQL, SQL, opportunity, or closed deal. Do this assessment for all marketing channels, such as paid social, Google Ads, display advertising, affiliates, conferences, or other sources.

Again, there are common stumbling blocks to conducting this assessment. The most common is that marketers have multiple customer segments, and the deal values vary considerably in scope. Selling products suitable for the SMB segment (small and medium sized businesses) and selling to enterprise companies (very large companies) will require different thinking.

In a monthly pool of 100 leads, if 40% of leads are low value (non-qualified leads), 30% are Marketing Qualified Leads (MQLs) of high quality, and 30% are MQLs of smaller size, some simple math can express success for each 100 leads obtained. For simplicity, calculate the rough value of each segment and then take a weighted average. While not ideal, it allows marketers to move out of "analysis paralysis."

Table 3 shows the aggregate lead value broken down by lead quality. In this example, there are 100 total leads: 10% are large company leads, 40% are medium, and 50% are small company leads. The total lead value is the lead volume multiplied by the value per lead.

Segment	Monthly lead volume	Value per lead	Total value per month
Large company	10	$2K	$20K
Medium company	40	$500	$20K
Small company	50	$200	$10K
Total	**100**		**$50K**

Table 3: Aggregate monthly lead value

Best practice is to track each lead through the entire funnel and understand its value. The goal is to generate a more sophisticated model that ties lead value to eventual downstream revenue generation, while understanding profitability for each customer segment and marketing channel. Pragmatically, it usually makes sense to simply evaluate the quality of the leads generated using some kind of lead scoring or evaluation metric. When evaluating lead quality, consider the company size, the title of the person, industry, and other relevant factors. The initial sales discussion can also provide a qualification of some kind, which should occur almost directly after the lead is generated. In this manner, lead value can be quickly determined without waiting for a final sale that could take months.

Part 3

Conversion Rate Optimization – Team And Process

3.1 CRO: A Tough Team Sport

The challenges of growing conversion rates are somewhat unique within digital marketing. A single, capable digital marketer could drive millions of dollars in media buys on a platform like Google Ads, in contrast, CRO is a team effort. One of the biggest challenges is building the optimal team. The right team includes, at a minimum, the following members:

1. Conversion optimization strategist
2. Project manager
3. Web analytics expert
4. Market researcher
5. User experience expert
6. Copywriter
7. Front-end developer
8. Quality Assurance (QA) specialist
9. Statistical analysis and interpretation expert

While some of these functions may overlap, most do not. Market research, copywriting, design, and front-end development are usually very different skill sets. Brilliant designers typically are not inclined to look through lines of code, debug errors, or write compelling web copy; front-end developers typically cannot check the quality of their own work. Even if there is a single person that can perform multiple functions, most would not perform all functions quickly enough for rapid and continuous testing. Skill sets and execution are reasons conversion rate optimization requires a team approach, ideally with team members that are masters of their respective crafts.

The alternative to building a team is to hire an agency to perform the work. Almost all agencies will work on a fixed fee basis.

Even well-funded companies will have difficulty budgeting to recruit and hire a team to conduct A/B and multivariate testing. Indeed, the salary costs will exceed half a million dollars in most American markets, not to mention the significant investment in purchasing software and conducting the relevant market research.

With insufficient resources, software, and talent, digital marketers will be challenged to pursue best practice conversion rate optimization. Digital marketers are busy. Juggling traffic acquisition channels, paid search, organic search, display, social, email, marketing automation, site updates, and internal meetings is multitasking of the highest order. The addition of a complex task, like conversion optimization, can easily be overwhelming and often ends up deprioritized.

3.2 Sample Size – Tests Only Amazon Can Run

There are two levers that drive quicker test results: the volume of conversions on a site and the size of the impact of a test (effect size). Larger volumes of conversions increase the velocity of testing by allowing a quicker path to statistical significance in a test. Simply put, more traffic means more tests. Furthermore, higher levels of traffic also permit testing smaller effect sizes: Amazon can test very small changes to its site experience given the millions of transactions per day. The classic example of difficult to measure test is button color change, which requires massive amounts of traffic. With fewer conversions on a site, testing becomes challenging, and the effect sizes (conversion rate lift) of a test must be larger in percentage terms in order to be measurable. Statistically, it is difficult to detect anything less than a 5-7% lift in conversion rate with sites that have fewer than 500 – 1,000 conversions per month.

For smaller sites, it is best practice to bundle a set of changes together in order to lift the conversion rate on the site, rather than attempting to get a small lift in conversion rate for a single change to a page. For sites with fewer than 100 conversions per month, it is difficult to measure statistical significance outside of very large increases in conversion rate. Sometimes measuring statistical significance is challenging, even for high-traffic sites, but volume adds to the ability to measure statistical significance.

Sample size issues often skew our perspective on customer data. Imagine that a new burger joint opens up in your neighborhood, and the first three customers walk in and do not order fries. It probably does not mean that french fries should be dropped from the menu, but rather that there is a statistical issue related to small sample size. You can easily get a streak of people that hate french fries, or encounter a series of customers who have a specific taste preference. A few hundred customers worth of data would be required before restructuring the menu. Even then, there can be hidden customer tendencies that require deeper analysis. Imagine if your most loyal customers, or your highest spending customers, had particular taste preferences. You would want to know this before changing the menu.

In cases where there are few conversions on a website, techniques such as user experience testing and advanced user sessions for qualitative customer feedback can be helpful. While these studies yield interesting insights around user behavior, they are not best practice A/B tests. A/B tests are regarded as the gold standard in measuring results in a similar manner to a scientific study; they control for outside factors using the random assignment of individuals to two groups. In this manner, all factors outside of the test are controlled. If your traffic doubles due to an increase in organic, PR, or paid traffic, or because of a sale, promotion, or product launch, the traffic all gets randomly assigned to each of the two groups, and the impact of these changes is reflected in both the test and control groups. We can have confidence that what is being measured is the change on the 'B' versus the 'A.' Without testing, there will always be a question mark regarding the conversion rate impact of a change to a site, even if it based on solid market research.

There are data sources that can give marketers an edge. For example, customized predictive analytics can fast track results and rapidly identify opportunities for revenue growth. Using predictive analytics can help eliminate some of the guesswork from testing. Not every test will succeed, and that is the principle behind building a testing and experimentation culture. The industry average is only a 10-15% success 'win' rate at best.[5]

The variability in test success is extremely high. Some teams obtain no wins in their first five to ten tests and give up. Teams with a thoughtful, systematic process may have a higher win rate. In general, there is a declining probability of additional test wins

---

5   Based on interviews with testing teams.

over time as a site is enhanced and optimized: early test wins tend to be larger, whereas later tests have smaller impact as the site becomes more optimized over time. Using hypotheses to increase the probability of success is best practice and reduces potential errors in testing.

3.3 Hypotheses Fast-Track Results and Reduce Errors

When trying to understand how changes to the web or mobile experience influence customer behavior, we use a best practice A/B test which has statistical limitations and potentially errors.

- Type 1 error is a false positive; that is, we see a positive test result that is an error and should be negative.
- Type 2 error is a false negative; we see a negative result that is in fact a positive test result that should be implemented.

For these reasons, we should always test strong hypotheses, concepts, and ideas that we know should have an impact on user behavior. If we guess that a call to action should be "talk to sales," but we have no research to support this, and then we test and find it increases conversion rate 2%, when someone suggests an alternate to this wording, we will be very tempted to second-guess the result. If, through user testing, we found that people want to understand more about our best practice implementation, and we test the "learn more about implementation" call to action with success, we will have a strong conviction to keep it on the site. We may retest these concepts at some point, but for big winners, we will likely remain convinced for the long term. As much as possible, use hypotheses and limit the guesswork in testing.

Typically, teams come up with a series of hypotheses that can be tested after research is conducted. The testing can be done a few different ways. If we obtain five good insights from customer analysis, each could have five different design or copy changes that should be tested. We therefore have 25 concepts for testing from these five insights. With customization and personalization, the number of test permutations multiplies, so we should prioritize tests with the largest potential first.

3.4 Organizational Challenges

Practically speaking, there are significant organizational challenges in executing a testing program within any company, and these challenges likely increase with the organization's size. That is, for larger companies, there are typically bureaucratic hurdles that make gaining approval for any change to a website difficult. Key stakeholders often include corporate marketing, branding agencies, product marketing, management approvals at various levels, legal, regulatory, and compliance. Compliance in industries such as financial services or pharmaceutical products or healthcare are particularly onerous and should not be underestimated. Despite the potentially large opportunity from conducting best practice conversion optimization, teams may find that they run a few tests and that those tests will be limited in their scope by the various stakeholders. Walking these stakeholders through the competitive risk and opportunity size is imperative when attempting to win these individuals over to a testing and experimentation mindset. Once people realize that their business' success is tied to the success of the conversion optimization program, they are more likely to help align their functions around a testing mindset.

Digital marketers often have much more latitude and less organizational overhead when optimizing landing pages. These pages have fewer stakeholders involved, are often controlled by the marketing function, and can be an excellent, low friction area to start testing. Once data exists in support of a testing and optimization program, marketers can then share this data internally and gain traction for a broader experimentation effort. Again, continually demonstrating the return on investment and competitive necessity of the exercise will help educate other stakeholders that are unfamiliar with the process.

Part 4

Neuroscience And Data – Secrets to Conversion Optimization Success

4.1 Battle of the Apes (or Customers)

Every good marketer starts with the same question: who is my customer, and what do they really want? Conversion optimization is no different. In order to understand how to boost conversion rates, we must understand our customers, what is motivating them, and what causes them anxiety with respect to our offers. Unfortunately, the task is not as easy as it sounds.

It has been long established that human beings are genetically similar to other primates. It follows then, that human beings are remarkably similar to each other on a biological level.

However, human beings perceive themselves and the world in a unique manner. You may ask a neighbor who she is, and she might reference her heritage, identify her religious background, upbringing, and family history. More conversation might reveal a passion for helping autistic children and how these aspects of her journey have influenced her life.

The fictitious neighbor is just one of numerous possibilities. Despite human beings being genetically similar, our experiences and thought processes can differ considerably. This varied experience shapes our perception of the world, and part of this is how digital properties are experienced.

By understanding our customers more deeply, we clear the path for systematic, hypothesis-based testing. Integrating this customer understanding with the website data on where customers drop off on the path to conversion will yield the most power in a testing program. This will help prioritize the concepts with the highest likelihood of increasing conversion rate, as well as targeting web traffic that is most easily influenced and valuable. This prioritization is the quickest path to conversion optimization and competitive dominance. A customer centric approach is key to any marketing effort, and conversion optimization is no different.

4.2 Emotion, Habit and Rational Behavior

It is tempting to believe that people will behave rationally and act in their own best interest. However, as any experienced marketer knows, people have very different sets of motivations for their actions and do not always behave rationally. For example, consider the purchase of a hat. There are two hats that are both made in Vietnam, but one has a brand or logo, while the other does not. One may be considerably more expensive due to the branding. The issue is the same in the B2B world; consider a SaaS (software as a service) company that sells a product that monitors web activity. There may be some companies that manage to sell this SaaS product despite the existence of Google Analytics, a free alternative that essentially obviates the need for this product. This is not to say there are not minor benefits to these products, but the perceived value is not necessarily rational.

Sticking with the SaaS subscription example, there are lots of reasons why companies are able to charge fees to small customers who are not aware of free options or alternatives that are a fraction of the price. None are rational in the context of well regarded, inexpensive, or even free substitutes. One scenario might be that a company has developed a strong emotional connection with the decision maker. If the company effectively expresses some differentiation for the product being sold over the cheap or free version, it can increase the probability of a sale. If the company has done a good job, it should be well positioned to renew business when the subscription nears its end or when the time for a repeat purchase occurs.

How a product can make you feel is often more important than its features and benefits. Consider a product facing intense online competition for traffic and customers. Company A prominently displays its product's features and benefits on the landing page. Company B displays feature information, but there is also a clever use of testimonials that make the brand seem more fun. While fun has nothing to do with product selection, making people feel good when reading web copy is always beneficial. I recall a clever startup with a testimonial saying that the product should be delivered on the wings of a Pegasus, with the quote signed by the founder's father. No matter what business a company is in, placing the visitor in an emotionally positive frame of mind can have a direct impact on conversion rate.

Another irrational but intrinsic factor is the concept of habit. Some buyers avoid sales conversations despite the fact that some can offer phenomenal deals or free advice; the interaction with the salesperson can always be managed by the buyer. Other buyers are the opposite, they auto fill their information along with their cell phone number whenever a request is made, not critically assessing the impact. While this may be a harmless habit, filling out random internet forms can cause massive disruption to the individual. Each form fill may lead to endless phone calls, personal information being resold, as well as an email inbox being bombarded with follow-up information.

Often, the biases customers have are unconscious. For example, when selecting candidates for a job, there is an inherent bias towards selecting men's resumes, despite there being female applicants with equivalent qualifications. Failure to recognize this inherent bias may negatively influence a decision.[6] Similarly, selecting younger, more attractive applicants over less attractive or older applicants, ceteris paribus, may be an unconscious choice. The processing occurs at a subconscious level for those who would never consciously select candidates based on anything other than qualifications. The same unconscious biases hold true when people are using a website.

---

6   Steinpreis, R. E., Anders, K. A., & Ritzke, D. (1999). The impact of gender on the review of the curricula vitae of job applicants and tenure candidates: A national empirical study. *Sex roles*, *41*(7-8), 509-528.

Consider another often irrational, large consumer purchase: a car. Even highly rational individuals are tempted to make purchases outside of their budget on the basis of some emotional reward. The excitement at the time of the sale seldom lasts, but the payments are impervious to this decline in excitement and persist. From a purely rational perspective, a car is a car. Most consumers would be sufficiently served by any vehicle that has adequate capacity and functionality for transport. However, consumers become very passionate about the purchase, often identifying the item with their ego. Luxury vehicles may be many times the price of the less expensive but sufficient, fully optioned alternatives. Many buyers opt for luxury options and feel fantastic about their choice.

Emotion factors into renewal of gym memberships for those aspiring to get into shape, even if they never actually go to the gym. Logically, cancelling should be a very easy decision because there is no point paying membership fees for an unused membership. The emotion behind this purchase is far more complicated. People may have guilt associated with how they look, the amount of weight they may have gained, and the lack of action taken to address this. Renewing a gym membership is an action that allows people to believe that their behavior may change in the coming year. Rather than taking a step back and assessing the reality that the gym membership went largely unused, they renew. They may be better off starting with a daily walk, but the action of renewing the membership allows the individual to believe that they will change and become fit.

We are used to thinking in terms of consumer purchases, but similar types of patterns exist in B2B transactions. Ultimately all customers are consumers that are at work, tasked with spending their company's money.

It is this thought process that permits a Silicon Valley based software company to have a median utilization of zero, meaning that half the "users" never use it; yet the company continues to be successful. Customers understand they should be using the software but cannot or do not, and the software remains installed. B2B customer motivations remain driven by emotion rather than absolute rationality. It is easier to renew a SaaS subscription than confront the attractive sales representative over lunch to explain why they are canceling. In front of colleagues or their boss, they do not want to appear to have made an error in signing up in the first place. Admission of poor decision-making on the part of the employee admits failure, whereas a renewal reaffirms the decision was correct. In another scenario, similar to a gym membership, the product subscription represents an uncompleted task or strategic initiative that remains relevant, although not executed. Customers cannot cancel software related to these objectives even if it goes unused. The actual cost of this unused software may be substantial for the organization, but it does not guarantee utilization by employees.

4.21 Human Brains Create Ideas Invisible to Marketers

Similar to habit, preconceived notions form a frame of reference. Many of these notions are ingrained from an early age. Nationalistic ideals have taken over the media in recent years with people holding very strong, opposing views on the same concept. Many professionals in digital marketing steer clear of these concepts in order to avoid any adverse impact on brands and campaign performance. Given how strongly ingrained nationalistic identity is, this behavior is prudent. Other ideas and concepts (e.g. religion, laws, and family) have formed the basis of modern society, inspired countless wars and lost lives; all in the name of an idea. Oftentimes, allegiance to concepts is used to inspired people.

In his book, *Imagined Communities: Reflections on the Origin and Spread of Nationalism*, Benedict Anderson explores the concept of nationalism. This concept is at the forefront of the current geopolitical environment. One of the inspirations for nationalistic identity is the rise of print capitalism. The mass production of print media, such as newspapers and books, and the ability to share ideas on a large-scale in a single, common, national language helped create the national identities of Europe.

In turn, this identity is sometimes supported by military activity and the sacrifice of millions of lives.

Consider another example of conceptual thinking: that the number three does not actually exist in any real sense. An insightful person had to figure out that numbers could be useful and that this concept of counting could also be practically applied. Numeracy, which we take for granted as part of the basic fabric of our existence, is a man-made concept and not a physical reality.

People's belief systems are often buttressed by the stories that we tell others and ourselves. In his book, *Sapiens: A Brief History of Humankind*, Yuval Noah Harari discusses how the entire history of mankind was shaped by story-telling and that much of what we see in history was driven by religious belief systems. He shows examples of monotheistic religions, drawing on practices of pagan religions. The stories of particular deities have become part of the fabric of a society and transpose themselves from one religion in a particular geography to another religion in the same geography. The story of the saint with the same name as a pagan deity from the same region is a striking example of how powerful story-telling is to the human mind. For practitioners of a monotheistic faith, transposing anything from a pagan religion would sound like an impossibility. Yet, we cannot deny how story-telling has influenced the structure of modern religion and our belief systems. The story of money and economics is one of the most powerful stories we have told each other, permitting strangers to transact globally with pieces of paper or plastic that we all believe hold value.

4.22 Applying Concepts of Influence to Design and Optimization

If these ideas and imagined concepts are ingrained in our psyches, to what extent are we taking these concepts and applying them to the digital experience? When we worked with the largest movie streaming service, we advised them on how to portray themselves outside of the US to place more emphasis on the local identities and culture and less on the American vision of family time and leisure. Even for smaller brands that are marketing products nationally, digital marketers can take the perspective that there are individual state level markets that will respond to marketing messages at very different levels.

For an e-learning product company, we had to customize the messaging for all of their landing pages down to the state level. While we initially thought we could do some customization that generalized to the entire set of landing pages, it turned out that each major state required some fairly significant customization. The state to state range of landing page sign up rate was 21% to 48%, a staggering difference of over 100% in conversion rate for *essentially the same product.*

If the product varies significantly from state to state, the margin of conversion rate performance can be even higher. Of course, as discussed above on the topic of statistical significance, we cannot look at state level performance and infer anything if we have too few conversions in the states being analyzed. We can also think about customizing the experience based on the customer segment and buyer persona.

4.23 Buyer Motivation by Job Title

When considering B2B sales, we often encounter buyers whose motivations are driven by emotion rather than rationality. For example, a company may consider a field service group as a cost rather than as a revenue center. However, this group may feel that being a revenue center is important, and so when positioning to sell to this group, the seller must showcase how they turn this cost center field service group into revenue generating heroes.

Staff members may desire to be seen as a contributor beyond the simple execution of the function suggested by their title. Table 4 shows pertinent examples.

Title	Example Job Activity	Emotional Findings To Be Leveraged in Conversion Rate Optimization
HR Manager	Recruiting	Wants to be seen as a team contributor, someone who not only builds staff but has a critical role in driving growth.
Procurement	Cost containment and negotiation	Wants to be seen beyond the function of contract negotiation. Seeks inclusion in the corporate team rather than being seen as a passive entity.
Accounting	Accounts receivable	Under pressure to deliver revenue, but functionally seen as a cost that does not contribute directly to sales. They are only on management's radar if things go wrong.
Marketing	Online Customer Acquisition	Under pressure to deliver leads to sales teams. The sales team often controls the internal dynamics. People in this role are stretched because of small team sizes.
Sales	Sales Development	Massive amount of pressure to deliver opportunities. Top performers are rewarded while the bottom are ruthlessly eliminated, leading to an atmosphere of fear.

Table 4: Examples of emotional purchasing triggers by buyer persona

The emotion driven insights in Table 4 may have implications when designing targeted conversion experiences. For example, if marketing software products for HR professionals, focus on how your product will help customers be perceived as driving contribution and cohesion and layer that into the site messaging.

That's not to suggest skipping over the mention of critical features. It is more to say that we need to include emotional triggers into the messaging within those features, nudging web visitors into a conversion. The initial nudge to conversion may be a lower hurdle, such as a webinar signup or whitepaper download with an email lead for your company. It can be challenging to focus on the most relevant features for customers in marketing communications, but well-targeted messaging will facilitate the emotion-centered conversion, rather than the logical "best feature set wins" mindset of many product teams.

It is important to consider buyer types differently. For example, if we are selling employee feedback and engagement software, we may have multiple targets within a company. In order to communicate the relevance of a particular product to a buyer's needs, pages can be designed to make it clear that the product addresses each function's interests and concerns (e.g., performance management and attendance), but also addresses the emotional needs of the buyer. When working for a leading telecommunications company marketing a phone service, my team created multiple buyer pathways on the website via changing the navigation on the home page and the follow-on web experiences customized for each persona. In this manner, each function feels validated and reassured that there is a strong fit between the offer and the customer need.

4.3 Fear Drives Decision-Making

Understanding emotion is critical in any sales and conversion process. As human beings, we tend to be more motivated by fear than incentivized by seeking gains, or greed, for lack of a better business term. Loss aversion is the human tendency to avoid losing something we consider to already be ours. Reaction is not as balanced as expected when it comes to decisions that involve loss and gain. Most people reject the chance to gain $100 if there is an equal chance to lose the same amount. It would logically be expected that the satisfaction one would get by gaining $100 would be equal to the dissatisfaction to losing the money, however, this is not the case. The subjective impact of losing is greater than the prospect of gaining. Scientists have measured this discrepancy and found that the fear of losing bears twice the impact of gaining similar amounts. Following this finding, most people would reject an opportunity unless the amount that could be gained is at least twice the amount that could be lost. In the end, we are simply predisposed to avoid losses much more than we seek gains.

Two interesting examples of this phenomenon are insurance and the lottery. People prefer to pay for insurance at a loss instead of risking a very large potential loss if not covered by insurance. Those who play the lottery take the sure risk of losing a very small amount in order to potentially have a very large potential gain. While the purchase of some insurance products and warranties represent sound financial decision-making, this is not the case with many of them, and almost no lottery or other similar gamble is financially rational.

There is no conclusive answer as to why losses have a disproportionate impact on decision-making. Explanations suggest that we are more sensitive to losses due to their association with negative emotions of fear and anxiety. This is supported by the fact that brain regions related to anxiety and fear (i.e. the amygdala and insula) are activated not only when experiencing loss, but also when anticipating it. In other words, the biological impact of a potential loss is similar to the impact of an actual loss. It is interesting to note that case studies of people with amygdala lesions suggest that these patients do not experience loss aversion.

Experimental results indicate that the neural network of the ventromedial prefrontal cortex, the anterior cingulate cortex, and the ventral striatum are activated when subjects are presented with a beneficial gamble and inhibited when they faced a gamble at a disadvantage. The research suggests not only that losses and gains are coded by the same mechanism, but also that there is a neurobiological substrate for behavioral loss aversion.

We can draw some conclusions about how loss aversion could influence website experience and design. People's decision-making can be guided by how offers are framed.[7]

When trying to guide people's decision-making, *the key point is to appropriately frame the offer*. Loss aversion is relevant in almost any digital sale or conversion; a few simple examples are:

1. Temporary discounts that customers could miss out on.
2. Features and benefits that involves reducing risk for a customer.
3. Scarcity of inventory of a product or limited availability of a service.

In each case, the offer is framed in a way that emphasizes the possible loss of opportunity. Potential loss must be stated in a clear and definitive way to stimulate a response. For example, use words like "don't miss out" instead of "gain" to imply potential loss of savings or benefits. Display a countdown clock to imply

---

[7] An interesting observation is that loss aversion impacts the risk involved in a particular situation. The Prospect Theory, described by Tversky and Kahneman (1979), suggests that people will make decisions based on relative outcomes rather than absolute outcomes.

a time limitation if it is relevant to the offer. Facilitate people's decision-making by providing simple binary choices. Another practical concept is using notifications or follow-up emails to stress the potential loss of leaving purchases unfinished and the loss of a special offer, in the case where a shopping cart is abandoned. Some of the better popup modals asking for the web visitor's email address offer an immediate discount and do not allow closing the box without clicking a button that says, "No thanks, I don't want to save money." That is definitely not something anyone wants to admit and plays directly into this sensitivity to loss aversion.

Scientists have discovered something they call the *endowment effect*. People tend to value something more highly than the market price of that item after they have received it as a gift. Interestingly, subjects do not report these items as being more attractive after receiving the item as a gift compared to before receiving the item as a gift. This likely means that the value comes from having the item in their possession and an aversion to giving up something that they deem to be theirs. When making offers, try to structure them so they are owned by the customer. A large e-commerce site ran a very subtle test telling members to "get your price" that resulted in a lift in conversion rate over simply "see pricing." Ownership and the endowment effect are interesting related concepts to loss aversion.[8]

Loss aversion is a powerful tool, but it should not be overused. It makes sense to present web visitors with a limited time offer, but follow through is important. Repeated use of loss aversion without actual loss of opportunity can lead customers to lose faith in your messaging. You will be perceived in the same light as "The Boy Who Cried Wolf." People are highly sensitive to companies and individuals that they perceive as cheaters. From a brain evolution standpoint, if you believe in the value of social interaction as a driver for survival, then this type of thinking makes sense. People that genuinely contribute to survival have value, but people that are a risk can threaten survival. Another reason to limit the use of loss aversion is to avoid a high degree of association with negative messaging. To maximize the benefit of loss aversion, use it in combination with other strategies that are consistent with your overall brand and marketing strategy.

As discussed above, loss aversion can take the form of a fear of missing out (FOMO), which applies directly to web decision-

---

[8] Kahneman, D., Knetsch, J. L., & Thaler, R. H. (1991). Anomalies: The endowment effect, loss aversion, and status quo bias. *Journal of Economic Perspectives*, 5(1), 193-206.

making. People have an inherent fear of missing out on limited opportunities. Persian rug sellers understand this phenomenon well. Their perpetual liquidation or bankruptcy sale has been a source of comedic entertainment in the media and anyone who frequently sees this tactic employed. Displaying a going out of business sign on an ongoing basis is implausible. While the stereotype is well-known, the rug sellers leverage the fact that the consumer believes they are going to miss out on a deal if they delay purchase. This can be effective despite understanding that the "sale" has been ongoing for a number of years.

The rug sellers understand this phenomenon and leverage their position, intentionally creating the impression that an offer reflects the last possible opportunity to save. They then further discount the price and reinforce that the deal on the table is the best deal possible. Of course, the seller communicates that the customer would be foolish to pass on this obvious opportunity to be a predatory buyer. Unfortunately for buyers, the rug dealer leverages these known tactics year after year. It is not unusual and may not be viewed as truly unethical. It is possibly true that the rug seller may have encountered cash flow issues and feels justified using the pretense of "liquidation" to advertise effectively. On the other hand, the consumer is not forced to make a purchase, and the door is always open. While online sellers should not seek to acquire this type of reputation, they should think very deeply about this form of motivation and how it could apply in an ethical fashion to their current offers.

4.31 Scarcity and Conversion Rate Optimization

These principles of loss aversion and fear of missing out may stem from our primal need to preserve scarce resources, such as food, during our hunter-gatherer phase (i.e. pre-refrigerators and grocery stores). Human beings are thought to be predisposed to always consider the concept of scarcity. We are also social creatures that fear missing out on trends that others may participate in. So, fear and anxiety related to loss or scarcity can drive purchasing behavior, or incentivize a potential customer to speak with a sales representative and eventually execute a purchase order. This concept is core to the customer psyche and thus should be factored in when considering the optimization of any digital conversion funnel.

The simplest examples on the web can be drawn from e-commerce: think of the travel sites that you have visited in the past. The concept of only a few seats on a flight or hotel rooms left at a particular price can drive a purchase. Many of these travel sites have well trained conversion optimization teams and understand that messages of scarcity nudge people into purchasing now rather than delaying the purchase, which often means losing the sale to a competitor. Sometimes the number of seats at a particular price may be limited, but the site may offer additional capacity at slightly different price points (e.g., $1 less or $1 more) immediately after the initial price and offer passes. In this example, they have created a simple false constraint on inventory, and a credible risk in the mind of the customer that they may have to pay more later if they do not act now. Often, this is coupled with a series of guarantees to assuage other concerns, such as a 24-hour risk-free cancellation policy. Again, these sites constantly try to reassure us against the risk in a transaction while communicating a potential loss of an amazing deal if action is not taken immediately. Most sites are not deploying these techniques resulting in lost conversions.

You can create the impression of scarcity in other ways; simply consider all of the different types of offers that drive leads or conversions and put a time limit or a quantitative limit on them. If you offer a free trial, this can often be recrafted to include a limited number of free seats for a specific time period or limited access to a premium set of features, or indicating that the trial offer is typically available under specific circumstances. If the customer does not participate now, they may not have access to a trial later. The trial can be tested in different forms or offered to customers in a particular geography, either in a particular state or country. Testing the free trial duration, three months versus six months versus one year, and measuring which offer triggers the highest number of conversions allows testing for the optimal configuration. Offers can be positioned and tested in an almost unlimited manner: bundled for a limited time with a purchase, a free trial offer made to a referred colleague or friend, various price points, offers to particular buyer segments, offers to specific sources of traffic, etc.

Of course, if the trial is always free because of the structure of your business model and competitive landscape, experimentation should be done cautiously, so as not to ruin the brand and relationship with the customer. Free products that subsequently require payment at a later point in the customer journey can create customer backlash, some of which can be harsher and longer-lasting than expected. That said, customers typically expect to pay at some point, thus, free trials can frequently be tested exhaustively in order to optimize for long term revenue. Often anchoring, setting the expectation of your price point, is helpful. If your pricing is high, there is no point signing up free trial customers that will never be interested in paying for your product or service. A high price point will cause customers to value your offer (see the section on pricing). Once customers perceive your offer as valuable and expensive, discounted offers will look very attractive relative to the initial price presented.

Some of the best known examples of this are TV offers on infomercials and shopping channels where goods are offered at a starting price and then heavily discount later in the show to rapidly close sales.

When making free offers, additional perceived value can be added by limiting quantities, introducing scarcity. If you are offering a webinar, you can limit the number of seats or make a special offer to bundle with the webinar for the first set of attendees. Of course, you can always expand the set of prospects by making the same or similar offer following the webinar, allowing customers to get access to your product or service. You can also allow prospects to obtain a referral bonus or offer a waitlist for another offer that may be running out, or could credibly appear to be running out.

These tactics can be deployed for almost any marketing asset or event, such as attending a conference with a special deal. With the expiration of the deal, an individual that missed out the first time will be more amenable to sign up on the second opportunity to receive a discount. Again, it is the fear of missing out in conjunction with the desire to be part of an exclusive group. Combining the different marketing messages into a cohesive story that represents your brand effectively can dramatically grow your sales leads and opportunities over time. There needs to be authenticity in your messages on scarcity, backed by a history of real time or product limitations, so think carefully about your strategy. For business-focused transactions, looking to the consumer world can help inspire the thinking process. Ultimately, your messaging must be on brand and professional, but your customers are simply everyday consumers who happen to be at work.

For sites that sell products, being clear that there are limits on quantities, as in the travel industry example above, can drive additional conversions. Showing products that have sold out in the past can be effective. Consider the example of a fashion site where a product is produced in limited quantities and turns over quickly. Many purchases are impulse purchases. Some products with a lower price point that target a younger audience are disproportionately occurring on mobile devices rather than desktop, and are more likely impulse purchases. Data suggests that these mobile visitors can be nudged into a conversion using the above discussed techniques. Just like the travel example, combining this with some reassurance on any common questions customers have can drive conversion rates even higher because people tend to outweigh the impact of loss versus gain.

4.4 Inclusion Drives Conversion

Studies show that people view exclusion from groups in a more negative light than admitted consciously. Human beings are very social, and inclusion is core to our instincts, so we perceive exclusion as a threat. An individual experiences exclusion as a threat at a similar level to a physical threat or pain. However, when it comes to workplace politics we understand that people remain outwardly stoic, particularly if exclusion is not explicit. The reaction can be observed and studied systematically.

There may be gender differences in the degree to which exclusion is perceived and experienced in the workplace. In either gender, it is a serious issue. To quote a 2017 Harvard Business Review article, "an absence of expected social engagement is a threat to a fundamental need; it signals that we are socially worthless and a bad fit for that very community that we depend on. This - as you may know from experience - makes being on the receiving end of ostracism acutely painful." [9] If we understand this phenomenon, we can start to address the issue in our digital marketing materials.

---

9 Robinson S.L & Schabram K. (2017) What to do when a colleague excludes you. *Harvard Business Review.* April 13.

EEG studies reveal that even minor forms of exclusion trigger emotions of sadness and anger. Consider the simple experiment of Cyberball, where participants pass a virtual ball among themselves.[10] Experimenters exclude a study subject from the passing game and observe the responses. Even this minor form of exclusion triggers a response from being excluded. This concept of inclusion into groups has been shown in a digital setting as well.

It turns out, people that feel sidelined or excluded from a group discussion feel threatened in an equally negative way in the digital world or physical world. The phenomenon was examined in the context of group text messaging. Researchers found that exclusion from a digital conversation, such as a group chat, can have a similar negative interpretation to being excluded from a physical interaction.

The concept has broad application. Consider a well-coordinated marketing conference where a company holds an event for its customers. Customers arrive from all over the country but do not know other attendees. Further, some of these conference attendees are introverts. They would prefer to be alone in an

---

[10] Williams,K.D. & Blair J. (2006) Cyberball: A program for use in research on interpersonal ostracism and acceptance. *Behavior Research Methods* 38.1 : 174-180.

office in front of a monitor or book, rather than amongst their peers. Engaging these attendees while they are in town and a captive audience is a technique used by the best marketing organizations. More than just permitting a sales interaction, it permits the hosting organization to offer up a community and a sense of belonging. All of this inclusive behavior results in customers having a stronger connection to your brand.

A sense of community is often enabled through online forums of various kinds, whether it is generalized learning, support, a blog or a discussion site. The possibilities are endless and tie in nicely with other marketing events or collateral, whether digital or otherwise. When following up via email, we can layer in personalized messaging that reference the community being developed. Systematic inclusion of individuals is a critical component of any marketing event or activity.

Some of the online and offline touchpoints that build towards a feeling of a community on the path towards a purchase and renewal or repeat purchase could include:

- Email messages (both templates and customized notes to the individual).
- Whitepapers, blog posts, and other marketing messages that add value to the customer group as a whole.

- Retargeting ads through display networks with relevant calls to action or offers for further information, depending on the stage of the buyer journey.

- Engagement in the community message boards that not only assists customers with the software purchased, but also offers content on other important topics relevant to their role.

- Building excitement and systematically reminding customers of the thought leadership the company stands for through messages from presenters at the company-run conference.

- Personal invitations extended by members of the management team to increase the engagement level and attendance at the conference.

- Sharing content based on presentations at the conference (e.g. video recordings, key speakers' thoughts, event successes, value to attendees, special events, etc.).

- Personal touches from the sales team to maintain relationships, check in on progress, identify concerns or issues, and understand how the product is being used.

- Interactions with internal team(s) to successfully onboard the customer.

- Ongoing training.

Of course, these interactions are focused on making sure that the customer feels excited about continuing to use the product or service. The purchase and renewal should be a foregone conclusion if marketing has done its job and sales has followed up appropriately throughout the customer journey.

Making customers feel like they belong to a group can help develop a very strong brand story and emotional connection with consumers. It creates high purchase and renewal rates, facilitates upsell opportunities, garners referrals, and extends awareness beyond the immediate customer base. This spillover effect is facilitated by social media sites, like LinkedIn, that permit the dissemination of valuable content that eventually drives followership. In this way, community can drive more sales opportunities by driving a higher level of conversion rate from prospective customers that believe in your brand. People do not just want to hear about your product and features; they also want to know that others are using your product.

4.5 The Power of Social Proof

Human beings are unique in the animal kingdom in our ability to collaborate at a very large-scale, and many scientists believe that this ability to coordinate is what makes us a powerful species. Scientists believe that it may be that our ability to collaborate and the brain's evolution are directly related. That is, that our survival may have depended more on collaboration than on being smart and figuring out the next tool. Even if that is not the case, the concept of human beings as social animals is very strongly supported. On the web, social proof can leverage this neurological underpinning and help ease the minds of prospective customers who are not familiar with a brand. Part of the goal is to prove that people and companies similar to them, or that they aspire to be more like, are using the offered products and services. There are a variety of techniques that can be implemented in order to achieve this goal.

Testimonials can be an amazing and relatively inexpensive way to quickly establish social proof. Even one happy customer can authentically communicate a story of enjoying the use of a product or service. Human beings respond well to other human beings. Of course it helps if the person giving the testimonial is a known personality, or similar to the customer visiting the site, but there are other methods of establishing credibility.

Testimonials from industry leaders

Industry leader testimonials establish credibility because of the personal background, company and position held by the individual. In B2B sales, it is the company name that drives credibility, given that individuals rarely have a brand that is as large and well-known as the company that they work for.

People may read the testimonial, but they may also assume that the testimonial is positive and gloss over the details and simply go on brand recognition. The phrase, "No one gets fired for hiring IBM," describes the fact that choosing a product endorsed by a successful company minimizes the possible risk.

Testimonials - target customer profile

Ideally, testimonials match the demographic of the prospective customers visiting the site. If prospects are mainly suburban mothers, then the testimonials and images should reflect this. If prospects are all HR professionals, then the credentials, experience, and comments should speak to that audience. A testimonial from an HR executive that attests to the fact that a piece of software was built by and for HR professionals, rather than IT professionals, speaks to the buyer. The endorsement will hold more value with the target audience.

Reviews

Another form of showcasing testimonials is to use a rating system from a relevant, known source. Google reviews, Yelp!, and G2Crowd are good examples of this. Even if your story is not strong, the large-scale utilization of these review sites implies validation. Ultimately, you just want to be part of the conversation and showing relevance by respected third parties. Establishing credibility, even with few but powerful reviews, is sufficient to start. Again, combining the reviews with some storytelling can lead customers to explore your brand.

Relevant logos

Sometimes, the most powerful endorsement is simply displaying logos. For example, a software company might showcase well-known customers' logos in marketing materials. Again, associating with recognized brands is validation. For a healthcare site, logos related to the education of the physicians or other employees or relevant accepted insurance carriers immediately convey trust. For a small e-commerce site, showcasing known brands will lift conversion rate.

On the other hand, some logos scare customers more than they encourage them. For example, a large organization may be scared away by display of small company logos, unless they are well respected and growing. A large company expects to work with companies that have experience with other enterprise organizations. Likewise, inclusion of logos exclusively from large companies will signal that products or services are focused on serving only large customers and scare away some smaller businesses with smaller budgets.

Logos of third parties, such as working partners or collaborative ventures, can also provide validation. Association with familiar brands conveys immediate recognition and confidence. If your company can showcase a dozen known logos, that effectively communicates credibility, even as a startup.

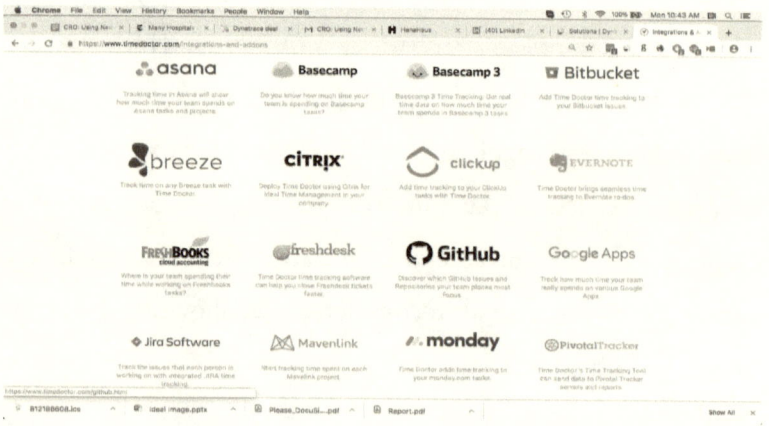

Figure 2: Time Doctor integrations, well-known companies provide reassurance to prospective customers.

Case Studies

Customer case studies dive into detail regarding how people and companies similar to your prospects use your product or service. Case studies are a great way to showcase results and other details that communicate value. Showcasing the value your customer service or success team, implementation, or thought leadership can provide richer detail than the product or services pages. A case study can build interest where the product alone would not.

Other media or PR, such as quotes or dialogue, can be the start of the customer journey. If a news outlet, publication, or other media is discussing how your company is changing the world, make sure the world knows about this by including a relevant quote and the logo associated with the media outlet.

An example of Atlassian using logos and numerical validation effectively (see Figure 3 below):

Figure 3: Showcasing the number of customers and some logos that resonate with customers will increase conversion rate.

Proof in the numbers

Growing up, I recall seeing every McDonald's sign counting the millions of burgers sold. This was an iconic use of social proof, communicating that x-million other people validated the product. If they enjoyed it, you will enjoy it as well. People want to know others are doing what they are doing, and often the sheer numbers tell the story very well.

Wealthfront effectively using numbers and media mentions (see Figure 4):

Figure 4: Publications that have showcased your brand can increase credibility and help drive conversions.

4.6 Emotional Needs and Attachment Driving Purchasing

It is often much easier to look at the market and understand the vanilla buying criteria that might satisfy customer needs. But this assessment ignores the very real concept that almost any decision made by a human being is emotion-centered. If an employee comes to work feeling overworked, tired, under-appreciated at home, and irritated after a two hour commute, that will impact how they make decisions. It will affect how they view different images and copy, and how they make a final buying decision, tipping them towards or away from a conversion.

A parent shopping for an online tutoring service or exam prep course for their child may have a vision for the child's life, impacting the visuals and copy that pave the way to the final conversion. What they see in reminder emails, cart abandon offers, and what other parents are saying impacts their buying framework for decision-making. There may be something deeper that can be tapped into by showing the vision of the future.

For some parents, their dream is for their child to enter the medical profession, law, or engineering. Other parents want their children to be happy and tend to exert less influence, celebrating the individual and the concept that anything is achievable. There may be opportunities to segment the experience and create specific user journeys as customer preferences are better understood over time.

Highlighting the number of exam prep questions or other bland criteria may not be as effective as combining these facts with emotion. In particular, we are looking for conversion triggers for someone that is "on the bubble." It is these people that are the focus in conversion optimization; they are the customers that can be nudged towards a conversion and have a significant impact on conversion rate. People who have already decided to buy do not require further consideration. Someone who has never purchased anything online is highly unlikely to convert to a customer no matter what their need is for your product or service.

Researchers discovered that personal finances and relationships can intertwine with decision-making. If an individual feels insecure about their personal relationships, they may have a higher tendency to make material purchases to compensate and lift themselves emotionally. Potential customers may substitute security in their personal life with a decision to buy. According to Beijing Key Laboratory of Experimental Psychology's Ying Sun and colleagues, those who desire money and material things generally have had experiences where their emotional security was threatened.[11] There are obviously degrees to which this is occurring on an individual basis. Going on a shopping spree after experiencing some form of emotional distress is commonly referred to as "retail therapy."

Some individuals are less secure about relationships and are more susceptible to influence; people with lesser degrees of insecurity are less easily influenced. From a web conversion standpoint, the focus is on how to fulfill the security and stability needs that the customer may be missing.

While focus on website conversion optimization is important, support for customers at a personal level will connect your brand and your customers at a human level. If you are a customer service oriented company, make people relate to you by speaking in a way that they understand. If you have examples of how you have helped people, as discussed in the section on social proof, make sure you showcase those examples. A larger and more personal commitment that is sincere and builds customer relationships is more emotionally appealing. Most websites have enormous opportunities to tell their stories in a way that

---

11 Sun, Y., Wang, L., Jiang, J., & Wang, R. (2018) Your love makes me feel more secure: Boosting attachment security decreases materialistic values. International Journal of Psychology.

more clearly conveys the personal commitment they make to their customers. Showcase their outstanding customer service, guarantees, warranties, and other policies that back up these commitments. New customers want to feel they are picking the right group to become a part of, and the service and security you provide can support the storytelling on your site.

4.7 Brain Shortcuts – The Neuroscience of Priming

Think of priming as a neural shortcut. If people have been conditioned to see the color red their entire lives in the context of warning and stop signs, chances are high that this will translate to the conversion world fairly directly (the red button color typically has a small but negative impact on conversion).

Take the example of virus scanning software companies using the symbol of a shield in their branding. This is precisely the kind of mental association that one can use to quickly deliver the mental shortcut that immediately conveys a message and image of the service or product being offered. In this case, the physical shield represents protection despite the fact that in the digital world there is no physical protection; it is simply software. Even the name of a company can be an opportunity. Consider the name HealthVault. Clearly the people at Microsoft that created this product understood that a key customer objection to sharing personal health information was security, and they integrated this objection into the naming of their new product. The image of a vault is a secure physical image, one that physically does not apply to digital data, but one that clearly describes the importance of security to a user.

An internet security company handed out condoms at a conference. The association of protection with the brand in an unrelated but provocative way helped create a long standing imprint in recipients' minds. By framing up your product or service and discussing it in a manner with which you wish to be perceived, you can shape the nature of follow on discussions and behavior with respect to purchasing. If your main differentiator is service, discuss the white glove approach to onboarding customers or installation; tell a story and make the concept stick. People are open to suggestion. A well-known study showed that participants would walk more slowly when presented with words related to being elderly than when presented a series of unrelated words.[12] The mere suggestion of being elderly affected the outcome of behaviors. Similarly, when primed with the concept of God and religion, people were more willing to donate money to strangers, compared to neutral or no priming controls.[13] Another study showed that subliminal presentation of a national flag for only 16 milliseconds can prime specific

---

12 Bargh, J. A., Chen, M., & Burrows, L. (1996) Automaticity of social behavior: Direct effects of trait construct and stereotype activation on action. Journal of Personality and Social Psychology, 71(2):230.

13 Shariff, A. F., & Norenzayan, A. (2007). God is watching you: Priming God concepts increases prosocial behavior in an anonymous economic game. Psychological Science, 18(9), 803-809.

responses to political attitudes; in particular, it strengthened the nationalistic tendencies and polarized polling results on issues related to negotiations with other nations.[14] As stated earlier, nationalistic tendency is ingrained in each of us from an early age; consider how powerful the branding of the red, white, and blue is when marketing a product. Mortgage companies, tax filing services, and car dealerships routinely use this association as a quick mental link to their own brands.

There are three main types of priming: perceptual, conceptual, and associative:

1. **Perceptual priming** is based on physical qualities like color or shape.
2. **Conceptual priming** is when two concepts have a similar meaning.
3. **Associative priming** is like conceptual priming, but concepts connect independently of their meaning.

---

14 A series of experiments that show that subliminal exposure to one's national flag influences political attitudes, intentions, and decisions, both in laboratory settings and in "real-life" behavior. Hassin, R. R., Ferguson, M. J., Shidlovski, D., & Gross, T. (2007). Subliminal exposure to national flags affects political thought and behavior. *Proceedings of the National Academy of Sciences, 104*(50), 19757-19761.

The role of priming in decision-making is a matter of controversy. Some scientists raise the possibility that priming is effective mainly due to the complete isolation of other environmental cues in test environments. In a real life situation, priming may be mitigated by other factors.

Testing demonstrates that, done correctly, priming works to increase conversion rates and influence users' decisions. It can guide visitors to consider and execute a purchase. Web copy that associates a brand with other well-known, expensive brands, primes visitors with high expectations of quality and service; giving high price points on the website or implying that the product or service is expensive with associative primes will facilitate customers eventually purchasing at a high price point. Alternatively, given that customers expect to pay a high price, they may be more likely to buy when an offer is made with either a real or perceived discount. This ties together nicely with the concepts discussed in the pricing section and anchoring expectations in line with the desired outcome.

When possible, prime to familiarity and create experiences that are in aligned with customer expectations in your industry. People enjoy familiar environments. In fact, they sometimes turn down better alternatives to stick with familiar concepts.

Americans, for example, prefer shopping at franchises and chain stores, despite the possibility of better experiences available elsewhere. When faced with the decision of staying with a known option or experimenting on something new, most people opt for the known option, perceiving it to be safer. As an example, for companies with less well-known brands, testing the more prominent display of known logos will test positively on product pages. The logo drives the user to feel reassured of their purchase. This test will have a larger impact for more obscure e-commerce companies selling well-known brands. When considering the user journey, make sure the brand and style is consistent; often, tests of new designs of specific web pages fail when there is a gap between the expected look and feel and the actual experience. When in doubt, survey other large brands that shape people's expectations. At the very least, make sure your web experience is consistent. This makes it easier on the visitor and causes less mental fatigue.

Consider the visual symbols that can support the claims that you are making, and use them as props in the customer journey. Consider the universally accepted perceptual primes that can guide users towards taking the desired actions. Turning buttons into arrows that guide users to the next step in the customer journey is a subtle prime that can be combined into an overall optimization strategy. Describing offers, products, and solutions in the context of something that users already understand can be very effective. Note in Figure 5 the arrows used on the buttons to indicate to users to take the next step in the buyer journey.

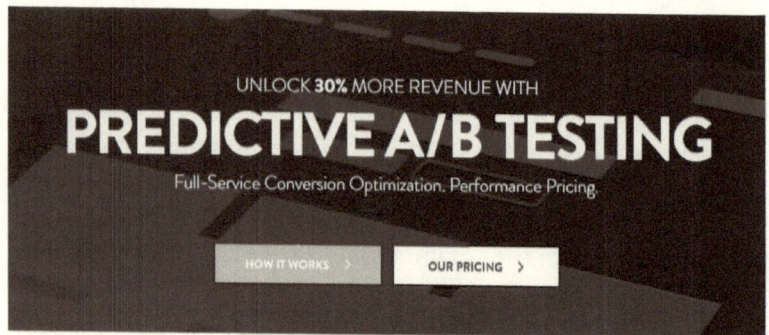

Figure 5: Using arrows as a universal prime to nudge visitors into action.

Priming is not a silver bullet. Avoid accidental priming such as using words that provoke negative emotions. For example, never say, "we will not steal your personal information," in a sign up process. Rather, say something positive about your policy and how you protect data if that is a key objection. I recently received an expensive reactivation mailer from a meal delivery service that stated, "now with reliable delivery." The message implies that there were delivery issues in the past, which is a negative for a company delivering perishable food products. Using negative phrasing will focus the buyer on the risk. It may be honest, but customers instantly make the negative association.

Priming depends on the audience. Personality and prior experience play a crucial role in the mental connections people make. Always keep the target audience in mind when creating messaging. Users should feel that their experience is natural. Lastly, do not over-influence. There is a lot of web content that attempts to flog buyers. However, over-stimulation reverses the intention of priming.

Part 5

Introducing Personalization

5.1 Personalization - A Structured Approach to Conversion Optimization and Segmentation/Multivariate Testing

Imagine meeting someone at a gathering and learning that you both share common interests, share a similar educational and cultural background, and you have similar goals and values. Chances are that you will like this person because of this commonality.[15]

Your circle of friends probably appears to be more similar than different from you. When we do not know someone, we tend to assess their abilities and personality by appearance. Most of the time, people tend to have a lot more in common with the same gender and similar age groups.

Multivariate testing is best practice to measure the true potential impact of personalization. A multivariate test is like an A/B test, with multiple groups in each of the 'A' and 'B' arms of the test. Consider the example where the traffic is split so that men and women receive different experiences in both the 'A' and 'B' arms of a study, essentially resulting in four groups instead of two.

---

15 Montoya, R. M., Horton, R. S., & Kirchner, J. (2008). Is actual similarity necessary for attraction? A meta-analysis of actual and perceived similarity. Journal of Social and Personal Relationships, 25(6), 889-922.

Implementing personalization testing in this manner requires a large volume of conversions. Without this volume, there are usually measurability issues related to limited sample size. If best practice multivariate testing is not possible, consider user experience testing where feedback on different web pages built for different types of customers can be powerful. Selecting an image because an individual in marketing likes it is different than selecting an image because users will respond better based on data, and some data is better than none. A consumer research study can give an unbiased insight into design that will convert optimally.

Consider ethnicity, gender, age, and other demographic features of your target customers. An easy example is testing the response to strong, gender-specific images between men versus women. If you are targeting middle-aged females with a family in a suburban setting, the assets you use will be different than for millennial females in urban centers. Understanding who your customers are, who is "on the bubble," and the defining tests based on this can be challenging. When done with large segments of visitors, personalization can drive significant additional conversions. This works as well for individuals as B2B customers.

If a company is displaying Americans on their Latin American landing pages, that is a mismatch. It can create confusion or disassociation for customers in Latin America; adjusting this would likely increase conversion rates. Both consciously and unconsciously, Latin American visitors will question whether the service that appears geared toward Americans is the right one for them. There is the subliminal bias against people that look dissimilar to ourselves and a preference for those that are similar to us. This bias is not something that a potential user group is going to report, so it may go unnoticed.

Emotion-centered content does not apply to your different market segments equally. The cute kittens may help with some segments of your traffic but not others. Optimally, each market segment is considered separately.

Consider a car rental company that targets different market segments. Their strategy allows for personalization of the digital customer journey in order to optimize for conversion of each market segment. Larger categories of customers for the rental company may include:

1. Geography - booking location
2. Geography - destination location
3. Business traveler
4. Leisure travel
5. Car size - large
6. Car size - small
7. Date of travel

Using relatively large categories for segmentation avoids statistical issues in testing with small groups (see earlier discussion on sample size). For each of the categories, we can test for different features: benefits, promotions, copy, and images that enhance conversion rate.

Considering each category separately, Table 5 represents tests that may provide valuable data.

Segment	Example	Test
Geography - home location	Detroit	Feature domestic vehicle examples.
Geography - destination location	Hawaii	Feature upsell to convertible car.
Business traveler	Booking from corporate traveler	Remove discounting promotions (may be less price sensitive).
Leisure travel	Booking to warm destination	Feature upsell to convertible car.
Car type large	Booking full size car	Feature upsell to small SUV.
Car type small	Booking a small car	Feature deals and promotions related to price more prominently.
Date of travel	Booking during major holiday	Feature upsell to small SUV.

Table 5: For a car rental company, example market segments, and specific tests that can be run for each segment.

The next step in testing becomes even more specific. Table 6 outlines how to combine individual behaviors, preferences, and market segments together to fine tune the personalization experience, while keeping in mind the sample size limitation of testing.

Scenario - multiple parameters	Test example
Date & destination: Long trip during Easter weekend in FL with small SUV (family vacation)	Push size upgrade and display discounted pricing for trading up during checkout.
Destination, days of the week and traveler type: NY to LA 2 day booking weekday as a business traveler	Unlikely to be price sensitive. Show offers for size upgrades, minimal discounting.

Table 6: Specific combinations of market segments present additional opportunities for targeted testing.

A systematic methodology for implementing a personalization program is important. The first step is to consider the most relevant segments of visitors that are coming to your website. Depending on the type of site and product or service categories, you may have multiple segments (as in the car rental example), or you may have a fairly homogeneous group of visitors.

Designing a custom experience for each major buyer type may be influenced by other factors and customized further. For example, if the acquisition channel involves different Google keywords, each landing page experience should be customized to the keyword and market segment. Similarly, Facebook traffic should be customized for the audience segment. In particular, specific offers, copy, and imagery should be consistent with expectations and should also be consistent for that specific user throughout the site. Think broadly about influencing each stage of the buying journey: early and late stage prospective customers typically need different experiences, and the customized messaging can be layered into all marketing messages.

Even with traffic that is not segmented by audience of some kind, there are plenty of smart ways to personalize the experience. This can be done in a highly automated fashion using sophisticated personalization tools and third-party data or by simply making segmented paths abundantly clear. The latter leaves the impression that each individual segment is valuable and relevant to the company. It also provides a means for visitors to clearly and quickly navigate to the area of the site that aligns with their market segment, interests, and requirements. Oil and gas executives see themselves differently from people in the hospitality and travel industry, so having different user experiences for each industry can greatly enhance engagement. Likewise, male and female consumers clearly have different shopping preferences.

Embracing the various customer segments and their preferences will validate the relevancy of their online experience.

5.2 Evaluate Whether Personalization Is Worthwhile

Personalization may be a lot of work. There are ways to evaluate if the investment is worthwhile. One is to consider the total value of each customer segment and the expected return from investing in optimizing the customer journey. This means returning to calculations to figure out what each one percent improvement in conversion rate is worth to your company (see the earlier section on lifetime customer value and the funnel analysis section below).

Part 6

Data-Driven Decision-Making in Testing

6.1 Funnel Analysis and Drop Off

Within almost all website analytics packages, exists the capability to view where web visitors go on a site, and where they exit or drop off. One of the most basic tactics is to carefully analyze which customers are abandoning the site and where, and then attempt to diagnose why this is occurring, structuring tests centered on these issues. The analysis can be conducted a number of ways; one method is to systematically look through each channel of customer acquisition. That is, look at Google Ads, social, organic, email, and affiliate traffic separately for example. You might take this a step further and look at individual keywords or specific campaigns in order to diagnose more accurately where there are opportunities for conversion lift.

Some simple math can very quickly help you prioritize your list of conversion opportunities. Take your volume of conversions for the particular landing page or conversion path and the total value of each conversion and multiply them together to get the total value of the opportunity. For example, if a landing page has 300 conversions per month, and the value per conversion is $100, then there is a $30K value per month (300 conversions × $100 per conversion). A 10% lift in conversion rate is worth $3K (10% of the $30K) per month. That is $36K per year ($3K lift per month × 12 months) in impact from a 10% increase in conversion rate. Keep in mind that pages that have below 100 conversions per month are difficult to test unless the effect size is very large.

$$\textbf{Baseline Value} = (\text{Volume of Conversions}) \times (\text{Value per Conversion})$$

Using the above formula, a lift percentage can be applied to quantify the value of an increase in conversion rate in any funnel. Systematically go through your various paths to conversion and conduct this simple math to find out where the largest opportunities are. If you are looking at a paid media campaign and funnel, consider using the return on advertising spend (ROAS) number or cost per conversion as a metric for value instead of conversion rate percentage. ROAS is the revenue generated from a conversion event divided by the cost associated with that conversion.

$$\textbf{Return On Ad Spend} = \frac{\text{Revenue from a Conversion}}{\text{Cost per Conversion}}$$

Essentially, one needs to consider the cost per conversion and compare this to the value of a lead, download, or other conversion event. You should be able to calculate the cost per conversion and then look to improve that metric. Prioritize your testing based on the cost per conversion for each acquisition channel multiplied by the number of conversions from each channel.

Lastly, if you can find an expert, they can estimate the potential opportunity to increase conversion rate for each landing page or conversion path based on their experience or by utilizing predictive analytics. Using the potential opportunity for conversion improvement, you can then reprioritize the list of conversion opportunities based not only on the size and value of the funnel, but also the potential opportunity to improve conversion rate.

6.2 "The Price Is Right"

One of my all time favorite topics on business in general is pricing optimization. In economics, there is a concept called demand elasticity. Essentially, the theory outlines that there is a relationship between the price of an item and demand; typically, as the price for an item rises, the demand for that item drops. Figure 6 shows an example of a demand curve where demand drops consistently with price increases.

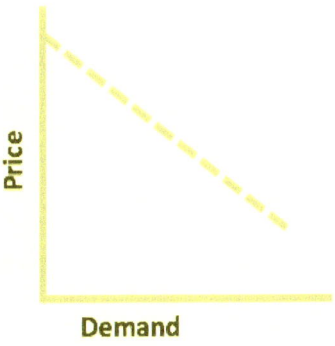

Figure 6: Demand drops linearly with price increases

Let's take an example like the price of apples at the grocery store. If the store raises the price of apples from $2 per pound to $3 per pound, there may be a drop in demand proportional to the increase in price. The amount that this varies is called the elasticity of demand for this item. For some items, volume may not shift much with price increases; indicating inelastic demand. That is, sellers can increase prices and not lose many sales.

Items for which demand fluctuates with price are considered to be more elastic. Of course, testing may reveal that there is not a smooth demand curve. Let's look at an example analysis: if the price of a pound of apples increases by a few pennies above $2, or maybe even 25 cents, there may be no impact on the demand of that item at all. If that is the case, the grocery store is leaving 25 cents of profit per pound of apples on the table when it sells the apples for only $2. Essentially, demand is said to be inelastic between $2 and $2.25 per pound.

This concept is easily portable to the web. In all situations where there is potential inelastic demand at higher prices, the sellers of those goods should likely raise prices. The impact on profits can be massive because each penny of additional revenue has no additional costs and would drop straight on the bottom line. If a pound of apples costs the seller $1.50, and the store sells the apples for $2, then the profit is $0.50. However, if the store sells its apples for $2.25, and there is no change in demand, the profit on the apples increases by 50%, from $0.50 to $0.75. Imagine increasing profits by 50%; this is the power of testing pricing.

Smart companies understand that there is enormous opportunity to increase profits through price optimization. The concept can get fairly complex and analytical in nature because there are limitless combinations of factors that can shape the price of an item. The goal is to optimize price for each scenario and segment in order to maximize profits.

There are ethical and legal considerations for pricing. Executives have been prosecuted for predatory pricing behaviors that harm the consumer. For example, in price-fixing, competitors conspire to raise prices in unison, limiting competition and increasing profits. Competition is healthy for markets and consumers and keeps pricing in line with demand while driving innovation. Regulators prosecute executives that violate the laws regulating free market principles.

Online marketers can experience a different kind of backlash. For example, if a company attempts to maximize profits by offering different prices to different customer segments, there is risk of backlash, even if no laws are broken. It is easy for consumers in different states, or certainly in different audience segments, to discover they are offered different prices. That can lead to a public relations nightmare which might destroy, or heavily damage, the reputation of a brand.

Ironically, in retail, offering different prices at geographically separate brick and mortar stores is a common practice. This makes perfect sense, as the cost to operate a store and a consumer's willingness to pay can be dramatically different in different places. The expectation that products and services should be the same in each city does not exist at the brick and mortar level. Online, consumers can become enraged when they discover a brand is pricing a product dynamically.

Despite the risk of consumer backlash, online retailers sometimes choose to dynamically price products based on multiple factors such as location, device type, viewing history, and other segmentation criteria. Brands may not admit to it, but price optimization is occurring, sometimes at a very large-scale. Be sure to weigh the benefits against the risks.

Even something seemingly benign, such as the offer for free access to site content with a follow-on request for payment, can be met with a negative reaction. Of course, consumers and businesses now expect that many free trials end in a request for payment, information collection, or automated billing cycles. Even if it is expected, lack of transparency at the outset can risk customer resentment when request for payment arrives. We should not restrict testing offers, but any testing process on pricing should be approached carefully, keeping in mind that money is a sensitive topic for customers.

Given that pricing represents such a large opportunity, and the online experience permits extensive testing opportunities, it is worth exploring perception and pricing research.

6.21 The Neuroscience Of Price Perception And Testing

Scientists from the California Institute of Technology and Stanford University have studied the impact of price on the perception of the quality of wine. They found that the stated price of sampled wine influenced the way subjects rated the wine. It also influenced activity in an area of the brain associated with perceiving pleasure.

Antonio Rangel had 20 volunteers tasted five wines, ranging in price from $5 to $90. The study volunteers were asked to evaluate the quality of the wines, and fMRI (functional magnetic resonance imaging) was used to scan their brains during the tasting process. The study subjects stated that they preferred the more expensive wines, and that these pleasant experiences were correlated with increased activity in pleasure centers in the brain. That is, they preferred the $90 wine over the $5 wine, but also the $45 wine over the $35 wine, and this perception was very real to the participants.

Volunteers' fMRI revealed that the medial orbitofrontal cortex (mOFC) showed higher activity during the tasting exercise when the subjects reported more pleasure. Rengel and his colleagues told study volunteers they were sampling five wines, though in actuality, they only sampled three. Some of the differently priced wines were actually the same wine, with only the pricing being different. In a blind taste test done as a follow-up study, in the absence of prices, the study subjects reported that the cheapest wine tasted the best.[16]

The study demonstrates that increasing price can increase the perceived value of your products and services. People consistently value higher-priced items over lower-priced products or services. In the study described above, the only driver for perceived value was price.

In development of online experiences, we have the full latitude to tailor the customer journey and communicate value. We can tie higher prices to increased profitability while making customers feel like they are getting the best product on the market. Most people have had the experience of purchasing a cheap product and wondering if it were the same quality as the more expensive item. Buying an expensive item is no guarantee there is any real difference compared to a less expensive item.

---

16 Plassmann, H., O'Doherty, J., Shiv, B., & Rangel, A. (2008). Marketing actions can modulate neural representations of experienced pleasantness. Proceedings of the National Academy of Sciences, 105(3), 1050-1054.

Pricing on a website can be structured so that there are lower and higher priced offers on the same page. This can be coupled with features and benefits that increase the perceived value of the offers at the higher price points. At the same time, these features and benefits of the differently priced items may not change the practical utilization of the product. Offering a premium version of the product or service is critically important to segment the market and maximize the profit of an online purchase.

Pricing pages are generally the most frequently visited pages on websites. People intuitively go to this page after exploring and discovering what they need to know about the product. One of the most common and simplest updates to a pricing page is increasing prices. This can take many forms and must include framing the offers in a light that makes them appear to be adding tremendous value. Ideally, of course, the premium products should add meaningful value, but that is not a necessity to segment the market and charge more to groups that have an expectation to pay more for value they perceive. To be clear, the ideal strategy is to increase the perceived value by both increasing price points as well as communicating all of the other features and benefits that increase a customer's willingness to pay for a higher tier offer.

To frame an offer optimally, we must understand who is visiting the site, what their intent is, and how they are evaluating competitive offers. Knowing these audience segments, we can structure a demand elasticity analysis using multiple factors to arrive at the optimal price point.

The simplest example is a single product site and a single price point for this offer. We can test different price points and measure demand at each one. The goal would be to figure out the optimal price for a product on the demand curve. We might migrate offers up the price and perceived value curves to make comparisons, as well as calculate the economics and track the results over time. Our target is to aim for prices that are at least as high as the perceived value we generate for customers, allowing for profit maximization.

The simplest test is to A/B test different price points to examine the drop off, or test different offers and structures. The pages for each of the tests should be identical except for the price, isolating it as the variable. From these results, you should get a good idea of the profit maximizing price point. Of course, this is a very simple example with a single product offered at a single price point. More often, tests include multiple price points for different versions of the same offer.

Each product permutation will have its own distinct set of characteristics that clarify the reason for different price points. Clarification of these differences avoids cannibalization, a term used to refer to the reduction in sales of one product due to a lower priced product from the same company. For example, if we sell a $50 per month plan as a discounted, introductory offer, we need to be careful that this does not reduce the sales of our $100 and $200 offers. The analysis of various pricing strategies and the change in demand of one product based on price changes to another product, also known as cross-price demand elasticity, can become fairly complicated.

The exercise gets still more complicated when we consider that price sensitivity can vary when customers purchase more than one product. In some transactions, a customer could purchase hundreds of products and would have very little sensitivity to price adjustment, especially for lower priced products that represent a small portion of the total purchase. Consumers typically compare the highest price products among competitors. Quite often, the situation leaves substantial opportunity for marketers to optimize profit on a per transaction, rather than on a per product basis.

If simply increasing the price of an offer increases the perceived value, then creating a positive experience of your brand can also positively affect a customer's perception of your offers.

From a traditional marketing perspective, the key to this strategy is that one must understand how to effectively segment the market. Customers that can discern the value and are willing to pay for higher priced products should not be tempted by lower priced products. It helps to define customer segments very clearly and then tailor the solution to that customer so that they see the specific, relevant benefits of a product in their pricing tier. If a specific target audience appreciates the value you bring, a higher willingness to pay will naturally ensue.

Another simple method to increase perceived value is to name product offers differently. People have consistently perceived more value when a product has a more elaborate name. For example, artisan bread is perceived as tastier than regular bread, even when there is no real difference between the two breads. This has been shown in many consumer studies.

Of course, combining perceived value with valuable features is the most powerful combination. Studies consistently find that higher priced products carry a higher perceived value. Interestingly, enterprise (large business) customers will often object to using a lower priced product simply because they do not believe that it will be sufficient for their company's needs. Again, just like the wine study, people believe the higher priced product is better.

In cases where prices are higher than competitors' prices, in B2B transactions requiring a salesperson, a worthwhile test is to hide all pricing and drive people to a lead form with a call to action that clearly states that the pricing details will be shared as a next step: a sales meeting. This meeting gives you an opportunity to describe why your product is better and of higher value before losing the customer based on the displayed price.

6.22 Pricing, Segmentation and Upselling

The relative price and value of a purchase can greatly influence the outcome of a conversion. For example, a warranty sold alongside a high value, high price purchase can greatly influence the overall profitability of a transaction.

With many products, there is an option for some kind of guarantee or service offering for support. This add-on feature may have high perceived value based on fear of loss. As a consequence of fear of loss, customers have a high willingness to pay, even if the actual risk is small, and the level of actual support may be trivial. Offering this type of add-on can tremendously enhance the profitability of a sale, given that the risk to the seller is low and should not inhibit the sale.

Let's consider an example familiar to most of us: a consumer purchasing tires. At the time of purchase, the individual may have suffered a tire puncture and entered the first available tire shop. Upon reaching the counter, she is pitched the additional purchase of a warranty, and because the price point is relatively low in comparison to the purchase of a tire, she is likely tempted to believe that this is a good investment. The salesperson likely has some tactics that position the investment as worthwhile. The warranty may have a very high level of profitability relative to the tires; often it is one of the most profitable items sold in any transaction.

Online, this transaction takes on an entirely new life. We do not have the luxury of a stranded customer in our waiting room, with a flat tire, and essentially no immediate competition. Online, customers are free to surf hundreds of sites and purchase wherever they would like. For that reason, it is incredibly important to consider the path to purchase, understanding that add-on items should not distract the customer from the final transaction. For example, if a $5 add-on is causing people to reconsider their entire purchase, or price compare the $5 add-on when the main purchase is $200 or more, this can cause a massive revenue loss. If 100 people are making a $200 purchase, and we create an add-on that is $5 that 10% of the customers buy, then we generate an additional $50 ($5 purchase × (10% x 100)). However, if this causes even a single customer to become distracted and not complete their $200 purchase, then the $200 loss outweighs the $50 gain by a factor of four. People easily get distracted from completing their purchases; a risk that can be avoided with large purchases in particular.

6.3 What Drives Willingness To Pay

Need is the biggest factor in increasing a customer's willingness to pay. Consider the willingness to pay for gasoline when someone is stranded on the side of a highway. In e-commerce transactions, consider the last-minute purchases made on Valentine's Day or before an anniversary. Customers have fewer options and will make a purchase quickly. Gifting is a high intent category with high conversion rates. When someone is sending a gift, it is often for an occasion, and that requires immediate action. Similarly, a customer may not be able to wait when replacing an inkjet cartridge if there is a deadline to meet. However, in this example, the high degree of price competition and transparency in product relevancy reduces the seller's profitability. Need can drive willingness to pay, but it does not give the complete picture on the subject. Thoroughly understanding intent can allow us to outperform competitors in both ad targeting and conversion rate.

6.31 Differentiated Offers Command Value

Your offer should be differentiated from your competitors to the greatest extent possible. Of course, almost any improvement or feature may be a welcome bonus for customers, whether they ever utilize these features or not. In that way, each feature has a potential impact on willingness to pay. As customers constantly evaluate products to compare attributes, an original approach can sometimes give you an edge.

Anyone that has visited a mattress factory understands the similarity between mattresses and the likely massive exaggeration in potential differences among various spring mattresses sold by retailers. These retailers benefit from a lack of transparent methods with which consumers can compare options. With online sellers such as Amazon, Casper, and Tuft & Needle aggressively entering the mattress space and offering risk free trials at price points well below typical retail, consumers can now benefit from direct comparison and competition. The same concept is true of many private label products sold next to their branded counterparts on grocery shelves and online stores; often private label products are exactly the same, and sometimes produced in the same factory as the branded product. The branded product appears differentiated and thus commands a higher price point.

6.32 Presentation Driving Conversion

In an interesting study, scientists compared three conditions:

1. Displaying the actual object.
2. An image of the object.
3. Text describing the object.

Their findings indicated a 40-60% higher willingness to pay when the actual object or image was presented, compared to text description.[17] In the context of web design, it is not possible to present the actual item. Despite this, using large, high-quality photos can improve conversion rate.

This concept is not necessarily restricted to physical goods; digital goods can also benefit from this principle. A short video of what software looks like or a conceptual rendition of the software that communicates key features and benefits, such as ease of use, transparency, reporting, data sharing, and collaboration results in higher conversion rates. Figure 8 is an example of the use of images to convey messaging for a software company.

---

17 Bushong, B., King, L. M., Camerer, C. F., & Rangel, A. (2010). Pavlovian processes in consumer choice: The physical presence of a good increases willingness-to-pay. American Economic Review, 100(4), 1556-71.

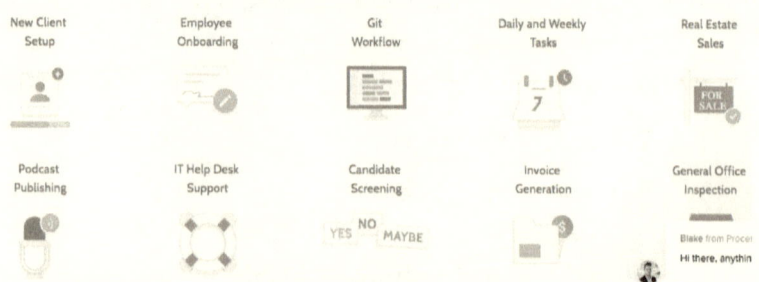

Figure 8: Process Street showing its features in a visual manner.

6.4 Neuropricing and Measuring Willingness to Pay

Assessing willingness to pay is difficult. Traditionally, researchers provide subjects with questionnaires and record responses. However, this method often leads to false predictions for two main reasons. Firstly, it is difficult for people to answer hypothetical questions such as, "how much would you spend on that?" If someone does not really need a service, they will not accurately evaluate their own willingness to pay. Secondly, it is frequently found that people underestimate the amount of money they would spend, as a sort of automatic bargaining strategy to get a lower price, even if they are part of a hypothetical testing group. It is simply a human tendency to seek the best deal possible.

More advanced testing can yield interesting insights based on electroencephalogram (EEG) studies. These studies monitor brain function in response to an offer. This new method assumes that our perception of value and willingness to pay are determined by the function of specific areas of the brain. Researchers use EEG studies to record brain activity when customers are presented with potential choices. The advantage of this method is that it avoids the bias that is associated with filling in questionnaires.

6.41 The Neural Mechanisms Implicated in Willingness to Pay

The expanding fields of neuroeconomics and consumer neuroscience attempt to address the question of willingness to pay. Studies of humans and primates seem conclusive that the prefrontal cortex is involved in the relevant decision-making. A 2007 study published in the *Journal of Neuroscience* highlighted the role of the medial orbitofrontal cortex (mOFC) and dorsolateral prefrontal cortex (dlPFC) in determining willingness to pay. The researchers used fMRI to monitor the brain functions of hungry human subjects while bidding on food.[18]

The model suggests that sensory information flows to the mOFC to determine the decision value, then passed to dlPFC and motor areas to affect decision-making. The same study group validated that the value calculation and choice execution were separate processes, with the former being served by the mOFC and the latter by the dlPFC.[19]

---

18 Plassmann, H., O'Doherty, J., & Rangel, A. (2007). Orbitofrontal cortex encodes willingness to pay in everyday economic transactions. Journal of neuroscience, 27(37), 9984-9988.
19 Plassmann, H., O'Doherty, J. P., & Rangel, A. (2010). Appetitive and aversive goal values are encoded in the medial orbitofrontal cortex at the time of decision making. Journal of Neuroscience, 30(32), 10799-10808.

In a more recent study, researchers used EEG to further explore the involvement of the prefrontal cortex in the determination of willingness to pay. Their results indicated that prefrontal cortex activity increased during the presentation of choices and decision-making on willingness to pay. They further demonstrated that it is the balance of right versus left prefrontal cortex activity that can accurately predict the subject's willingness to pay.[20]

Many of the most successful brands engage customers beyond the immediate purchase of a product or service. Research has focused on presenting users with opportunities for social interaction. These opportunities included posting a comment, tagging a friend, or participating in a discussion. These interactions increased a customer's willingness to pay, compared to a mere presentation of the content. The results also indicated that the best strategy is to create a "ladder of participation" by increasing the effort required for each action. The idea is that each rung of the ladder increases the commitment level of a study participant and, by extension, their willingness to pay. The ascending order of effort is crucial, without which the results do not hold.[21]

---

[20] Ramsøy, T. Z., Skov, M., Christensen, M. K., & Stahlhut, C. (2018). Frontal brain asymmetry and willingness to pay. Frontiers in neuroscience, 12, 138.
[21] Zalmanson, L., & Östreicher-Singer, G. (2014). Increasing willingness to pay through encouraging social participation - a web experiment. ECIS Proceedings 2014.

6.5 Leveraging Neuroscience

There are many A/B tests that have very small effect sizes. That is, their impact on conversion rate is very small, and they require large sample sizes in order to measure results. However, using advanced instrumentation, such as fMRI, offers a path to measuring these small, but real, effect sizes. There is evidence that human beings will be influenced by experiences below the level of testing on a best practice A/B test.

For example, a red color can often signal caution or cause a pause in the customer journey. When testing this hypothesis, an alternate color like blue that denotes professionalism could be tested. It may be difficult to measure and confirm this hypothesis during an A/B test for statistical reasons – the effect size is very small but it does exist. Of course, any changes should make sense within the context of a company's brand and style guidelines. Ideally, teams should make trade-off decisions based on empirical testing of design change.

Understanding how the human brain makes decisions and what science says about this could impact website design. To date, the field of consumer neuroscience has mostly focused on consumer decision-making in the offline world (think Palmolive dish soap or McDonald's). It can be challenging to connect findings from these studies to the field of digital marketing. Learning from this body of science can give insights into digital conversion.

6.6 Brain Imaging, And Conversion Optimization

It is easiest to consider the brain in two pieces. One is the "croc brain," the more basic from an evolutionary standpoint. The second is the higher level frontal cortex.

The emotion centers that drive all of the basic human emotions (e.g. desire, anger, fear) all come from the croc brain. Our ability to consider these emotions and decide what to act on occurs in the frontal cortex. As marketers, we routinely address what the conscious mind is thinking. This is relatively easy, in that we can interview, question, and observe people in order to find out what they are thinking. Unfortunately, the whole picture of human behavior must include subconscious decision-making, in addition to conscious thought.

An internal set of learned biases causes individuals to behave in a particular manner. It may not be politically correct at times, but our croc brains are constantly at work influencing our thoughts and actions. Large consumer brands and advertising firms understand this well. They use the latest in brain imaging technology and other measures of neural activity to observe the brain's reaction to different phases of the customer decision-making. They understand that measuring neural activity levels can enhance the study of consumer behavior. This knowledge can help marketers influence the outcomes of advertising campaigns, long-term brand perception, and increase sales.

For example, it has been observed that an area of the brain called the ventral medial prefrontal cortex vmPFC is involved with inhibiting purchasing behavior. Researchers also learned that playing music reduces this inhibitory effect and facilitates purchasing behavior. Leveraging this as we consider the multimedia nature of marketing online is important.

Consumer neuroscience has not always been broadly leveraged by digital marketers. Instead, studies of A/B and multivariate tests abound. There is no shortage of information suggesting massive conversion rate improvements from running the correct test on a site, generating the expected lift in revenue as a result. Often marketers attempting to obtain quick wins deploy these tests only to find that the results are not measurable. Even if the tests are based on sound thinking and the study of quantitative funnel analytics, as well as robust analysis, the tests do not yield conclusive results.

The issues discussed above outline the challenges inherent in any testing program. The core of what digital marketers execute against should be measurable results. That said, we should be augmenting empirical testing with as much qualitative information as possible. By keeping the brain science at the forefront of the design process, we can create a digital strategy to migrate customers towards long term advocacy, repeat purchasing, and referral behavior. In other words, create the ideal customer.

Neuromarketing techniques are often leveraged by consumer products companies. Some tools include eye-tracking (recording what captures attention), facial emotion coding (measures real-time emotional response), biometrics (e.g. heart rate), and neural measurements (EEG and fMRI). The authors of a Harvard Business Review article discuss how fMRI is a very powerful tool in studying the brain but is often underutilized because of cost and the limited access to machines.[22] This is echoed in my conversation with marketers who frequently have to make trade-off decisions when picking the tools they use because of cost and access.

---

22 Karmarkar U.R., Yoon C. & Plassmann H. Marketers should pay attention to fMRI, *Harvard Business Review*, (2015) November 03.

Concluding Thoughts

By thinking deeply about your customers, and endlessly seeking to uncover opportunities to connect the dots between customer needs and your brand, the path to increasing conversion rate and revenue will become clear. Look beyond the immediate metrics of digital conversion and consider how to build value in the minds of customers and then continually build that equity over time. Think holistically, like a sleuth, about customer behavior and human behavior, rather than limiting thought to online experience alone. By digging deeper into what is possible to test and developing a systematic method for understanding customer motivations, you will be equipped to develop comprehensive strategies for the entire conversion funnel, including experiments that can be tested empirically to drive results.

Acknowledgments

My journey into understanding how neuroscience connects to the online experience and website conversion optimization has been guided by many influences. I have worked alongside phenomenal people, each humble enough to share their wisdom. In turn, they helped me in the ideas discussed in this work. These people include colleagues, customers and others who challenged me to think deeply about the dilemmas customers face. Many of these customers pushed me and my team to higher levels of performance and deeper understanding of the challenges inherent to the complex world of online marketing. My mentors include professors and senior business colleagues who took the time to impart their wisdom and fast-track my learning opportunities. This work would not exist without the contribution from my editors and the help of research scientists who indirectly and directly contributed their thoughts and ideas.

No acknowledgement is complete without thanking my family, who supported me through a road less traveled, even as the journey becomes more challenging.

About the author

Dr. Ali Nasser runs a global digital marketing technology company. He and his team have worked with companies like GE Digital, Workday, NBAStores, Lowe's, Pepsi, and Maui Jim. Over the course of his career, he has been an entrepreneur and executive, and was a consultant at McKinsey & Company. He holds an MBA from the University of Michigan where he graduated with distinction, a Doctor of Chiropractic from CMCC in Toronto, and a degree in Biopsychology from the University of British Columbia. He resides with his family in Palo Alto, California.

www.ingramcontent.com/pod-product-compliance
Lightning Source LLC
Chambersburg PA
CBHW021818170526
45157CB00007B/2627